ADVANCE PRAISE FOR
A PRAYING CONGREGATION

"A congregation that is actively and authentically 'hanging out with God.' What a compelling image! This book is a profound and practical resource that pushes toward and enables that vision. In a culture with a real yearning and hunger for a more intimate relationship with God, this book is a gift for congregations and congregational leaders."

—Rev. Mary Armacost Hulst
Calvary Baptist Church of Denver

"This is an essential resource for pastors and leaders committed to deepening a congregation's spiritual life. The detailed instructions for small-group activities are not only user friendly but reveal the theological reflection of a deeply faithful person and the rich experience of a skilled teacher. Vennard's concise introductions to spiritual practices and forms of prayer will enrich the prayer lives of both individuals and groups. This book will help readers become open and available to the grace and generosity of the Holy Spirit."

—Joseph D. Driskell
Pacific School of Religion and Disciples Seminary Foundation

"This book is the work of a master teacher, and like all master teachers, Jane Vennard is clearly in love with her subject. She is in love with the honest, spirit-stretching questions people have about prayer. She is in love with the stunning multitude of ways people can engage in spiritual practice. She is in love with what a praying congregation can truly become. Drawing deeply from her personal experience, she leads her readers into the joy—and humility—of helping others discover the life-filling richness of prayer."

—Steve Doughty
pastor and author of *To Walk in Integrity*

"Jane Vennard adds another illuminating gem to her impressive body of work. What a wonderful gift to the praying world—a savvy, inspiring, wise, instructive reflection on how to gently lead a congregation into the life-changing practice of life-changing prayer."

—Patricia Raybon
author of *I Told the Mountain to Move*

A Praying Congregation

The Art of Teaching Spiritual Practice

Jane E. Vennard

THE
Alban
Institute

Herndon, Virginia
www.alban.org

The Alban Institute
2121 Cooperative Way, Suite 100
Herndon, VA 20171-5370

Scripture quotations, unless otherwise noted, are from the New Revised Standard Version of the Bible, copyright © 1989, Division of Christian Education of the National Council of the Churches of Christ in the United States of America and are used by permission.

Cover design by Adele Robey, Phoenix Graphics.

Library of Congress Cataloging-in-Publication Data

Vennard, Jane E. (Jane Elizabeth), 1940-
  A praying congregation : the art of teaching spiritual practice / Jane E. Vennard.
    p. cm.
  ISBN 1-56699-313-X
  1. Prayer—Christianity. I. Title.

  BV210.3.V465 2005
  248.3'2—dc22
                                            2005008204

            09 08 07   VG   3 4 5

For Capitol Heights Presbyterian Church

"*When the church is no longer teaching the people how to pray, we could almost say it will have lost its reason for existence.*"

—Richard Rohr

CONTENTS

	Activities	*ix*
	Foreword	*xi*
	Preface	*xv*
1	**Praying Congregations**	**1**
	Talking about Prayer	1
	Creating a Safe Environment	4
	Respectful Listening	9
	Freedom to Explore	15
	Becoming a Praying Congregation	21
2	**Learning to Pray**	**23**
	The Value of Memorized Prayer	28
	Teaching Others to Pray	30
	A Firm Foundation	34
3	**What Do You Believe about Prayer?**	**37**
	Primacy of Prayer	41
	Relationship with God	42
	Embodied Prayer	44
	Everything a Prayer	45
	Prayer and Action	49
	A God Who Listens	50
	The Mystery of Prayer	53
4	**Images of God**	**55**
	Old Images of God	56

	New Images of God	59
	Considering God's Power	65
	Divine Intention and Divine Interaction	67
5	**Praying All Ways and Always**	**75**
	Renewing Your Spirit	75
	Practicing the Presence of God	78
	A Rule of Life	80
	Accountability	88
6	**Becoming a Teacher of Prayer**	**95**
	Your Relationship with God	98
	Experiencing Prayer	101
	Teaching with Integrity	104
	Embracing Mystery	108
7	**Teaching Prayer Forms and Spiritual Practices**	**113**
	Intercessory Prayer	116
	Body Prayer	118
	Arrow Prayers	120
	Musical Prayer	121
	Centering Prayer	123
	Lectio Divina	125
	Gratitude	128
	Work and Service	129
	Praying Out Loud	132
	Going Deeper	134
	Afterword	*139*
	Notes	*143*

ACTIVITIES

1.1	Creating Safety	7
1.2	The Talking Stick	13
1.3	Spiritual Explorations	17
2.1	Memories of Learning to Pray	25
2.2	Prayer Questions	31
3.1	Beliefs about Prayer	39
3.2	Everything a Prayer	47
3.3	Answered and Unanswered Prayer	51
4.1	Healing Our Image of God	57
4.2	God Is Everywhere	63
4.3	Divine Intention and Divine Interaction	71
5.1	Renewing Your Spirit	77
5.2	Daily Intentions	81
5.3	Your Own Rule of Life	85
5.4	Finding a Spiritual Friend	91
6.1	The Compassionate Observer	99
6.2	Authentic Teaching	105
6.3	Alternative Lessons	109
7.1	Further Resources	135

FOREWORD

"What a great teacher!" My friend had just returned from a five-day retreat with Jane Vennard and, frankly, I was relieved. I had strongly urged his participation, and since he went with a fair measure of skepticism, I wasn't sure how he'd respond. His words not only reassured me—they also confirmed my sense of Jane's giftedness as a teacher, which also comes through so clearly in her writings.

Bringing just the right amount of theory and story, Jane offers considerable wisdom and guidance in this slim volume. Don't let the size fool you! Carefully chosen activities invite the reader to engage in what they are learning, and potentially this small book could occupy a teaching team for several months. The pay-off would be a congregation with a much more intentional ministry of spiritual formation, a ministry in which lay and clergy could share.

In the preface, the link is made to a Canadian study regarding the needs of mid-career clergy. Since the 1990s, considerable interest has been generated in spirituality, and many of us who attended seminary before or during this era felt poorly prepared regarding the rich traditions of spirituality and our own spiritual journey. More recently interest in spirituality has converged with interests in congregational development, making this book truly "cutting edge." More and more people are asking, "How can spiritual formation become something that's not on the periphery of the church but at the very center? How can the local church be a place that people look to for spiritual guidance and wisdom?" Here in this volume we hear a similar line of questioning: "How can I bring my own particular experiences, questions, doubts, and beliefs regarding spirituality into my local church? Is it safe to do so? Will there be people there who will both listen to me and have something to offer?" You can sense the urgency in these questions and the need for leaders and teachers to embody the answers in their own stance and ministry. That's why this book is so important.

Perhaps the single most important concept in the book has to do with creating a safe environment for conversations about prayer. Too often we have assumed that this was something we could take for granted. Unacknowledged as a place of great vulnerability, our spiritual lives and past experiences do not easily come to the surface. We are unconsciously more vigilant here than we even know, looking for signs from others that this relationship, this group, this congregation is a safe place for disclosing our tentative and unfinished relationship with God. Clergy leaders may project their own insecure faith on to their congregation, curtailing the richer possibilities for life-giving dialogue about matters spiritual. Those of us who are ordained will gain much from Jane's example of attentiveness to past experiences and timely self-disclosure.

Are there difficult and even controversial topics related to teaching prayer? We talked about how we tend to minimize the need for a safe environment to encourage conversation about prayer. In a similar way, we have underestimated just how much potential there is for conflict in spiritual matters. Think of the resistance to using a more modern translation of the Lord's Prayer and you get an idea of what's at stake. Teaching about prayer means addressing some of the most challenging matters of faith. Jane does not avoid these topics, but faces them head-on in her chapters on beliefs about prayer and images of God. Whether you agree with her theology or not, she models something very important for us—a willingness to state what we believe in a succinct and intelligible manner. My hunch is that she is able to do this because she has already established a level playing field. Her vision of "praying congregations" encourages everyone to be engaged in these essential matters. If congregations can engage in controversy regarding matters of belief about prayer, a certain transformation has already occurred.

While prayer practices have been encouraged throughout the book, in the last chapter Jane suggests some particular prayer forms. Her summary of each spiritual practice provides an excellent introduction, encouraging those who want to learn more. And while this chapter provides a helpful list for potential teachers, it comes after some very wise and insightful reflections in chapter 6. "Becoming a Teacher of Prayer" will seem like a daunting goal for many of us, but less so after reading what she has to say. In sharing her own story, she invites us to include our own hesitancy and humility when we teach, as a sign of our trust that ultimately it is the Holy Spirit who teaches these things.

Emerging from this book is a hopeful sign that congregations can embrace a ministry they have long neglected. Barriers of hesitancy and even fear can be lowered and much can be learned from one another. The congregation's raison d'être is confirmed as its spiritual life is rediscovered and nurtured into fuller flower. Something really beautiful happens when spiritual community breaks forth. While always tentative in a world of greed and violence, pentecostal possibilities for congregational life may not be as far away as we thought. At the very least we can come to value and learn from one another in congregational life, in a way we haven't always done.

—Jerry Haas
Director, The Academy for Spiritual Formation
Upper Room Ministries

PREFACE

In the summer of 2003 I received a call from my friend and former editor, Beth Gaede, who had recently read a Canadian study about the needs of mid-career clergy. This study found that many pastors identified a need for more skills or skill training in teaching others about prayer and spiritual practices.[1] "Is this something you'd be interested in writing about?" she asked. "A book on how to teach prayer?" I was intrigued, for teaching has been my calling for 40 years.

I began my professional life as an elementary school teacher. After eight years with fourth, fifth, and sixth graders, I left the classroom to teach continuing education programs for teachers at all grade levels. My focus was on the process of teaching and developing ways to help students become the motivated learners I knew they could be. I also attended to the teachers' attitudes and belief systems about teaching and learning, helping them to grow in confidence and follow what they knew to be good for the children in their classrooms.

Ten years later, after much loss and confusion in my personal life, I decided to enter seminary. I was not sure what my ministry would look like although I was fairly certain I was not called to parish ministry. As my studies unfolded and my faith deepened, I realized I wanted to continue teaching and to follow my interest in prayer and spirituality. I also felt called to the ordained ministry. In the United Church of Christ one does not need to serve in a parish to be ordained. With my love of teaching and my growing interest in prayer, I was approved for ordination to a special ministry of teaching and spiritual direction. In 1987 I began teaching prayer as adjunct faculty at the Iliff School of Theology in Denver.

Much of what I knew about the process of teaching I had learned when I was teaching nine- and ten-year-olds. Children do not let you get away with being inauthentic, redundant, or boring, so they forced me to find my creativity and to develop a personal teaching style. In the elementary school classroom I learned to trust myself in the art of teaching. When I thought about teaching adults I knew I could bring my knowledge about the process of teaching and learning to these new settings. I was unsure, however, about how to handle the content of prayer. Therefore, I simply began teaching the way I had been taught in seminary. I would present a prayer form to the class, talk about its origin, describe the method, and ask the students to practice the form and see what happened.

The students' responses to a variety of prayer forms, such as intercessory prayer, praying with scripture, body prayer, and centering prayer, were not at all what I expected. As the students shared I began to hear beneath their immediate responses to the spiritual practices traces of childhood experiences. "I couldn't even begin to use my body to pray," a student said. "I was always made fun of when I danced." Another student had a very negative response to the Eastern Orthodox practice of praying with icons. "I was warned about idol worship in my home church. That is what this form of prayer felt like to me," he said. "I loved singing my prayers," another student said. "It reminded me of praying with my grandparents."

Everyone likes some prayer forms better than others, and some spiritual practices seem to fit their needs in the moment.

But I realized that many people were not able to truly discern what method of prayer was appropriate for them because they held tightly to some preconceived ideas about prayer, often left over from early teachings in childhood. I also discovered that students would pray the assignment, but when the class was over, they were not so faithful in prayer. I came to realize that simply giving instructions on different forms of prayer and spiritual practices did not usually lead to a deepened prayer life. I needed to find a way to help adults prepare their hearts to receive the new information and then to integrate the practices into their daily lives. I began to wonder if they needed to uncover memories of the experiences that were influencing how they prayed today.

To explore this theory, I invited students to remember the ways they were taught to pray. I asked them to reflect on who taught them and what the specifics were. Were they taught by words or by example? Maybe they couldn't recall how they learned but realized they had been praying for their whole lives. From these memories, I invited students to begin to articulate their beliefs about prayer. Did they believe prayer worked, and if so what did they mean by "working"? Did they believe God wanted them to pray? What did they think happened in intercessory prayer? Identifying their beliefs about prayer often led to an examination of theologies of prayer. Was God a loving God who heard prayers with compassion? Or was God a judging God who punished by withholding answers to prayer? Did God listen to everyone or just to those who prayed "right"? As these questions were asked and the students struggled with their own answers, the teaching and learning changed dramatically. I discovered that when people became involved in these issues, the classes came alive. Exploring memories, reflecting, and sharing were ways of preparing their hearts to learn new forms of prayer.

This book is a result of those discoveries. It is about preparing people's hearts so they are ready to learn to pray more intentionally and in new and different ways. Individuals may prepare their hearts through reading the descriptions and stories about learning to pray and by completing the suggested reflections and exercises. However, the book is also designed for congregations. As important as an individual's prayer life is, it must be supported, acknowledged, and challenged by a loving community. Therefore, this book includes guidance for clergy and lay leaders who want to learn new ways to teach their congregations to pray.

I have placed the lesson plans in sidebars to make them easily accessible to those who will be using them and so they can be ignored by those who will not. I provide only guidelines so that teachers of prayer can infuse the lessons with their own spirit and creative ideas, discovering their own art of teaching others to pray. In the final lesson plan in chapter 6 I suggest a variety of ways the lessons might be woven together, combined, or extended depending on the setting, the size of the group, and the length of time available for teaching.

Chapter 1 describes what a praying congregation looks like. It tells stories about what can happen when a community not only prays together but becomes willing to explore its experiences, questions, and doubts about prayer. Chapters 2 through 4 guide individuals and congregations into recalling their memories of childhood experiences, articulating what they believe about prayer, and formulating their theology of prayer by discussing images of God. Chapter 5 explores the possibility of praying without ceasing. Chapter 6 invites those of you who are going to teach others to pray to look at ways you can be more authentic and effective in your teaching. The book ends with ideas and resources for teaching and learning specific methods of prayer once individual hearts and the heart of the congregation have been prepared. It also includes some suggestions for helping people overcome their fears of praying out loud.

I believe that God is calling all of us into deeper prayer and is longing for our congregations to become places of prayer. My hope as you read this book is that your heart may be made ready to strengthen your relationship with God through prayer. I encourage you to take your discoveries and struggles into community, so that others may be inspired to talk more about their own prayer experiences. When dialogue about prayer, as well as praying together, is an integral part of a community, that community becomes a praying congregation.

ACKNOWLEDGMENTS

I am blessed with a far-flung praying community, consisting of people who pray with me and for me, who talk willingly about prayer, and who continually ask evocative questions. I am grateful to their contribution to this book: Minnie Baldwin, Donald Bossart, Stephen Brackett, Brad Burgland, Rita Burgland, Joe Driskill, Trish Dunn, Ed Everding, Sheryl Fullerton, Beth Gaede, Margaret Hankins, Barbara Ann Johns-Schleicher, Margaret Johnson, Dottie Lamm, Chris Larsen-Rinquest, Jamie Laurie, Jim Laurie, Paul Laurie, Lou McCabe, Susan McKee, Mark Meeks, Kathy Mordeaux, Carmen Neafsey, Daniel O'Connor, Larry Peacock, Sharyl Peterson, Phil Porter, John Reamer, Steve Replogle, Macrina Scott, Diane Shields, Pat Shaffer, Bernadette Teasdale, Vie Thorgren, Kathy Turley, Jeanne Updike, Pat Vestal, Patti Waser, and Cynthia Winton-Henry. In addition to those named are many friends, hundreds of students, participants in prayer retreats, and those who come to me for spiritual direction. All of you have filled these pages with your stories, strengthened this book, and enriched my life. Thank you.

A Praying Congregation
Jane E. Vennard

- Creating a safe environment for conversations about prayer.
- Is this congregation a safe place for disclosing our tentative and unfinished relationship with God?
- Exploring memories, reflecting, and sharing were ways of preparing their hearts to learn new forms of prayer.
- Praying congregations are lively places made up of diverse people who are longing to take prayer seriously. In these congregations members want to learn about prayer, wrestle with hard theological questions, and learn from one another.
- Prepare the hearts of the people to receive instruction on prayer.
- When people experience their congregation as a safe place where differences are respected, a place where they are free to

explore, their hearts will be open in readiness.

- How do people know they are emotionally safe, that they will not be discounted, made fun of, or judged?

- To become a praying congregation, everyone must be free to share their deepest hopes and fears and to reveal what is most important to them.

- One way to begin creating a safe environment is to invite members of a newly forming group to remember a time when they felt safe in a gathering and to examine the behaviors that made it safe.

- Deep listening is the key to developing respect for others.

- One way to begin practicing listening to another's soul is to understand the differences between debate, discussion, and dialogue.

- In debate we are always trying to find a way to prove the other wrong.

- In discussion, we listen only enough to formulate our response.

- During dialogue, people agree to listen to each other with an openness to possibly being changed by another's idea, opinion, or story.

- We go into dialogue with the attitude that we might not have the whole truth. We are willing to be transformed.

1

PRAYING CONGREGATIONS

Praying congregations are not temples of holiness. They are not filled with mystics or experts on prayer. All the people do not sink into silent prayer as soon as they arrive at church. Their clergy and lay leaders do not tell others how to pray or what their relationship with God should look like. Praying congregations are lively places made up of diverse people who are longing to take prayer seriously. In these congregations members want to learn about prayer, wrestle with hard theological questions, and learn from one another. They are offered the opportunity to explore their prayer lives in depth, and their experiences and ideas are listened to with respect. In praying congregations everyone becomes eager and willing to talk about prayer.

TALKING ABOUT PRAYER

Most people in our congregations do not talk about prayer. They pray together in worship, and they listen to the pastor pray. Someone may open a committee meeting with prayer or say grace before a shared meal. Members of a prayer chain may receive names and concerns for which they are to pray. But very few people talk about prayer. They do not share their experiences, and they do not raise their doubts and fears. They seem to be reluctant to ask hard and fascinating questions: Does God hear our prayers, and if so, why doesn't God answer? Why does God seem to answer some prayers and not others? What if we pray "wrong"? If God already knows everything, why pray? What happens when two people pray for opposite things? Can I pray without words? What does it mean to listen to God? How do you do that?

I believe that many members of our congregations carry a huge number of wonderful questions about prayer that they are afraid to ask. Maybe they don't know who to ask or feel

The ministry of a praying congregation is to help people prepare their hearts for prayer.

they do not have the questions formulated well enough to ask them. Others in our congregations may be afraid to share their powerful prayer experiences. Their prayer time may have made them feel vulnerable, and they do not feel safe about sharing. They are afraid of being misunderstood or even ridiculed.

I also suspect that many people feel guilty about their prayer lives. They are not sure they are praying in the right way; they think they should be praying more; they compare themselves to others whom they see as "real pray-ers." These members avoid all conversations about prayer because they are afraid they will seem stupid, bad, or unfaithful.

All of these people need to be in conversation—to express their fears and doubts, ask their questions, and tell their stories of wonder. In fact, to have this conversation may be the reason many people come to church. George Arthur Buttrick, a renowned preacher, once said: "Pastors think people come to church to hear sermons. They don't; they come to pray and learn to pray."[1] If this is true, many of our congregations are not meeting their members' needs.

Sometimes when congregations do recognize these needs they will organize and offer educational programs, retreat days, or a series of prayer experiences, usually led by an outside "expert." Often these events are not well attended, and pastors and lay leaders think that their congregations are not really interested in prayer. I believe that the longing is there. The problem is that very little has been done to prepare the hearts of the people to receive instruction on prayer. Would I become involved in an intercessory prayer chain if I wonder whether this form of prayer works? Why would I attend a program on dancing my prayers if I had been taught that the only correct way to pray was on my knees? How could I learn about centering prayer, let alone begin to practice this prayer, if I have not explored the purpose of prayer? Would I want to learn new ways to become intimate with God if I hold an image of God as judgmental and punishing? Exploring these questions prepares the heart to learn how to pray.

The ministry of a praying congregation is to help people prepare their hearts for prayer—to recognize their desire to pray and help them explore these longings. Then they will be ready to receive instructions about different methods of prayer. The parable of the sower as told in the Gospel of Luke reminds us of the importance of preparation:

> A sower went out to sow his seed; and as he sowed, some fell on the path and was trampled on, and the birds of the air ate it up. Some fell on the rock; and as it grew up, it withered for lack of moisture. Some fell among thorns, and the thorns grew with it and choked it. Some fell into good soil, and when it grew, it produced a hundredfold (Luke 8:5-8).

Good soil is plowed and ready, moist and rich. When the soil has been tilled, seeds will take hold and sprout. So it is with the teaching of prayer. If the heart has not been prepared to receive, the information about prayer will fall on hard dry ground and never blossom. If we want to teach people to pray, we first attend to their hearts. When church members experience their congregation as a safe place where differences are respected, a place where they are free to explore, their hearts will open in readiness.

CREATING A SAFE ENVIRONMENT

We like to think of our churches as safe places, and most of them are physically safe. We have smoke alarms and accessible exits. We have plans for calmly and gently handling someone who becomes disruptive. We greet people at our doors with smiles and words of welcome. We are eager to make the church environment friendly and hospitable. But how do people know they are emotionally safe, that they will not be discounted, made fun of, or judged? How do they know that the pastor will not embarrass them by asking them to share before they are ready or by telling others things spoken in confidence? How do they know that the person sitting next to them will not ignore them or that a suggestion made or a question asked will not be laughed at? It is difficult to come together to worship God with open hearts and to discover community if we are afraid. It is also hard to learn when we do not feel safe. All good teachers know this and do everything possible to create a safe environment for learning.

Years ago when I was teaching elementary school I was determined to make my classroom safe and hospitable. The point I chose to focus on was name-calling, because I believed the threat of being teased or ridiculed created a hostile environment. The children were in the habit of calling one another "stupid," "dumb," or "ugly." I believed this meanness made students feel unsafe, so from the very first day of school, I made it clear that name-calling, any name-calling, was forbidden. It took the students a long time to realize that I was serious. They tested me and called each other derogatory names. "We're just teasing," the students would say. "We don't mean any harm.

Anyway, she likes it." I would let no excuse rest. I would let no name slip by my finely tuned ear. One day, after I chastised a child once again for calling another a mean name, she said to me in despair, "Why do you care so much? We do it on the playground all the time." I replied, "I cannot control your be-havior beyond this room, but I am determined that all of you will have one place in your lives where you are safe." I felt a collective sigh go up from the class. Somehow, that made sense to them. I heard very little name-calling the rest of the year,

> *It is difficult to come together to worship God with open hearts and to discover community if we are afraid.*

and when it did happen, another child would often step in and say, "You know that is not allowed in this classroom." With the absence of name-calling the environment became safe, and the students were more willing to ask questions and share their experiences. Their learning was enhanced.

Adults are not as blatant in their judgment and scorn as children. We usually do not call each other names, at least not directly. But we can behave in ways that bring a sense of danger into a group. We may ignore a comment offered by someone. We may discount it with statements such as: "We tried that and it didn't work." "Our church is not ready for that." "That would cost too much money." All those statements may be true, but offering such a response to a creative suggestion serves to make the one who offered it feel wrong, discounted, or excluded. If this kind of discussion continues, the one who originally spoke will either defend herself and begin an argument or will fall silent, offering little else. She may eventually leave the group. In addition, the others in the gathering who have witnessed the exchange will learn that this is not a safe place to speak from the heart. To become a praying congregation, everyone must be free to share their deepest hopes and fears and to re-veal what is most important to them.

As members gather to learn about prayer, they do not need hard rules to make an environment safe, but they do need to hear the topic of safety addressed. Everyone watches, wonders, and waits to see if a place is truly safe and feels a great sense of relief when the issue is discussed.

One way to begin creating a safe environment is to invite members of a newly forming group to remember a time when they felt safe in a gathering and to examine the behaviors that made it safe. As participants go through the process of remembering and then sharing the things that made them feel safe, they can together build guidelines to facilitate their present experience. Guidelines might include the need to listen carefully and not to respond immediately, to never discount another's experience, to hold all sharing in confidence, and to pray for one another in the time apart. The guidelines put forward need to be discussed to make sure everyone understands and agrees with them. People may need to ask some clarifying questions such as: "How often do we pray for one another?" "Is there a particular way we should pray?" "What if I feel discounted? Can I bring it up?" "Can I talk about my own experience outside the group?"

The way this discussion goes, how people are listened to, and how questions are answered does as much, if not more, to build safety within a group as the guidelines presented. When the leader is relaxed and open, giving time and respectful attention to the questions and concerns raised, he is not only telling participants that this is a safe group, they are witnessing and living in it through the verbal and nonverbal exchanges. Too many of us have been told that a situation is safe and the people are trustworthy only to discover to our dismay that it is not true. Have you ever been in a group where the leader says all ideas are welcome and then, when a participant offers an experience that differs from the leader's, she is discounted or

ACTIVITY 1.1: CREATING SAFETY

Time: 20 to 30 minutes

Materials: Chart paper and markers

Setting: Chairs in a semicircle so all can to see the chart

When members of a group participate in creating their own guidelines for making a group safe for everyone, they will take more responsibility for their behavior. You can create guidelines at the beginning of a class that will be used for the duration of the course. This activity uses participants' previous experiences in other safe groups to elicit ideas for their guidelines.

Evoking Memory

- Ask the participants to remember a time when they felt safe in a group. It may be a time from childhood or a more recent experience.
- Invite them to close their eyes and use their imaginations to relive that experience. Ask them to remember what made that group feel safe and to look for specific behaviors in themselves and others.

Sharing Experiences

- Allow participants to share their insights. Record responses on chart paper, being careful to use the wording presented or asking permission to alter wording if you feel it needs to be changed.
- Read through the final list together and see if anything needs clarification. Ask if there is anything on the list they would have trouble working within this setting.

Implementing the Guidelines

- Discuss together whose responsibility it will be to make sure the guidelines are followed.
- Either post the list or have it typed so everyone can be given a copy to keep.
- Make plans to review the guidelines periodically.

made to feel wrong? So we are careful and cautious. We test the waters; we wait and watch. Safety in any environment is built over time and is created when people not only talk about respecting others but show that respect through their actions.

Occasionally there are those in our churches who are so wounded that their behavior makes other people feel unsafe. Maybe they shout at those they disagree with or storm out of the room if they feel unheard. Sometimes they carry tales, engage in gossip, and break the covenant of confidentiality. We often think that if these people just left, we would have a safe group. We would like to send them off to do their own healing before welcoming them into the community. But what if a safe group is the avenue for healing? What if they cannot heal in solitude but need a group that accepts them unconditionally, even if their behavior is disruptive? As difficult as such ministry might be, praying congregations tend to the hearts of even the most broken among us. We treat them kindly and offer them the support they need. Those with more hidden wounds watch, wonder, and realize that if they expose their pain, fears, and doubts, they too will be accepted. They will be included, heard, and welcomed as valuable members of the group.

Respect is something that grows and develops; it comes from a deep inner place of insight and compassion.

Last year I was a guest preacher at an inner city church in Denver. This congregation has a number of programs providing care and food to persons who are homeless and chronically mentally ill. Many of these people attend a Saturday lunch program where, instead of going through a line for food, they are seated at carefully set tables while volunteers serve them. They love the church and are used to being welcomed. The Sunday I was preaching, two men from the program wandered into the service in the middle of my sermon, made their way to the front, and sat down. One man seemed particularly agitated, talking loudly and gesturing widely. The congregation tried to ignore them as I continued preaching. Immediately, with no visible alarm, the pastor of the church went over, sat down beside them, and gently placed his arm around the one man's shoulder. He leaned over and murmured softly into his ear. The man seemed to listen attentively, and I could see him slowly begin to relax. The pastor remained there throughout the sermon, his arm draped comfortably around the other man's shoulder as they listened to me together. A friend in the congregation told me that although she enjoyed my sermon, that action of the pastor's gentle hospitality meant more to her than a thousand words. In his own quiet way, he demonstrated the respect he had been advocating.

RESPECTFUL LISTENING

As much as we might hope our congregations are places where everyone feels safe, people cannot be commanded to respect one another. Respect is something that grows and develops; it comes from a deep inner place of insight and compassion. But even before I go into a new group and meet new people, I can proceed with the intention to treat everyone respectfully. One of the ways I can demonstrate that respect is to listen carefully when others speak.

I am often called to teach prayer in congregations where theologies and political opinions are different from mine. I have a tendency, as I imagine most of you do, not to hold in high esteem those other convictions or the people who hold them. When I enter such a place, I try to remember that I am called to honor strangers and treat them with dignity. I am also reminded that I am a stranger among them, and I desire to be treated with that same respect and honor. And so I go into that congregation with a listening heart. I listen to the language people use to articulate their faith. I listen to the passion they have for God and prayer. I listen for their personal prayer experiences. What do I hear under the words and the stories? The same longings as I have, the same questions, and the same need for affirmation. As I hear our similarities as well as our differences, I realize we are strangers no more. My respect for these people, their ideas, experiences, and lives begins to grow.

Deep listening is the key to developing respect for others, and yet we rarely take the time to truly listen. Instead of listening we assume that we know what the other person is saying.

Deep listening is the key to developing respect for others.

Rather than attending to what is beneath the words, we busy ourselves, formulating a brilliant response. We may even rush to finish another's sentence or attempt to answer a question that has not even been asked. We so often listen to others, and others to us, in this disrespectful manner that we have come to think of it as normal and appropriate. But if we have ever been truly listened to, we know what a gift that can be.

One hectic, busy, and stressful day I was racing through the halls at the seminary where I was teaching and a student called out to me. "Jane, how good to see you! How are you?" "Fine," I replied without thinking. "Good to see you too." Instead of being waved off by my abrupt answer, he gently stepped in front of me, looked directly at me, and said quietly, "Are you really fine?" I was surprised, a little taken aback, and finally grateful. This person was ready to listen. This person had clearly already been listening, for he caught my dis-ease and heard my frenzy. He really did want to know how I was. In a praying congregation, we do want to know how it goes with another's soul. So we ask, and then we listen.

One way to begin practicing listening to another's soul is to understand the differences between debate, discussion, and dialogue. A debate can be a formal event in which individuals or teams take opposing positions and through logic and strength of argument try to prove that their position is right and the other position is wrong. Sometimes a panel of judges awards points and one side is declared the winner. We may not participate in formal debates, but this model of communication is common in our culture. We speak to one another as if we were trying to win points and ultimately declare victory. In a debate we listen for weakness in the speaker's argument or for words that are not logical—for an opening, a chance to attack. In debate we are always trying to find a way to prove the other wrong.

A discussion is often a politely disguised debate. Although we may not use an attack mode, we listen only enough to formulate our responses. Before the person is finished speaking, we know what we will say, and sometimes we have planned out what to say after that, and then after that. In discussions, people often talk over each other, interrupt one another, and just wait until they can be heard. Not much listening goes on in such a discussion, and at the end people often feel frustrated. Nobody won, nobody lost, but no one was truly heard.

Dialogue welcomes silence—pauses between words, space between speakers.

During a dialogue, people agree to listen to each other—not with the intention of getting a point across, but rather with an openness to possibly being changed by another's idea, opinion, or story. We go into dialogue with the attitude that we might not have the whole truth. We are open to the possibility that someone else's experience could help us see an issue more clearly. When we enter dialogue we are willing to be transformed.

Dialogue is the preferred mode of communication in praying congregations. When we speak of matters of the heart, ask important questions about the nature of God, struggle with our doubts, and share our experiences of God's grace in our lives, we need people to hear us through. When we make ourselves vulnerable in these ways, quick responses are not helpful, easy answers are not welcome, interruptions break the power and passion of the sharing. Dialogue, on the other hand, welcomes silence—pauses between words, space between speakers. Silence comes into the group as a friend and companion to be embraced rather than an empty hole to be filled with words. In the silence we let the words and feelings of another's experience enter our hearts. We have time to consider what truth the story holds and how it may illuminate our own understanding. We also have time to see how we might respond with clarity and compassion. Our response then becomes an offering that the other is able to accept, reject, or simply take home to reflect on.

I experienced church members in dialogue about prayer taking time for reflection after hearing a moving story. I was interviewing a number of people at a large church that had an active prayer ministry and asked one of the participants to tell me about the prayer program and what he had learned from it. He talked about becoming involved in a program of intercessory prayer as well as meeting weekly with a small group for Scripture study and prayer. He told us how his personal prayer life had deepened through these experiences in community and how grateful he was to his praying congregation. I asked him how his life had changed since he became more involved in prayer. "Oh, my life has gotten much worse," he said. "I lost my job and my health insurance. My wife is not well, and my daughter's marriage is breaking up." He paused, and then he smiled. "But," he said, "I have the courage to face these difficulties, because I know, without a doubt, that God is with me. God does not make our lives easy or good. God gives us the strength to live our lives faithfully."

ACTIVITY 1.2: THE TALKING STICK

Time: 20 to 30 minutes

Materials: Some sort of stick that is light and easy to hold or possibly a small smooth rock, or any other object that is easily passed from one person to another. Simple writing materials for each participant and a bell or a chime will be needed.

Setting: Place chairs in a circle for five or six people. If the group is larger, divide them into smaller groups, each in their own circle with their own talking stick.

The talking stick is a tradition in some Native American traditions designed to help group members speak and listen to each other without interruption or cross talk. The talking stick helps groups in our culture practice dialogue.

Choosing a Topic

- The topic for the dialogue should be one of interest to all in the group and one that is open ended.
- Choose a topic that will engage the heart as well as the mind.
- The topic can be phrased in the form of a question such as, "When have you been truly listened to and how did it feel?" or "What has been your experience of silence alone or in a group?" or "What ways do you feel most comfortable praying?" A focused question is usually more engaging than a broad topic such as "listening," "silence," or "prayer."

Giving Instructions

- Explain that only the person holding the talking stick may speak. If the stick in not in your hand, you may not talk.
- When the person with the stick has finished speaking, he passes it to another in the group. Silence is to be maintained until the stick is passed.

- Members who wish to speak may hold out their hands to receive the stick. However, the one with the stick who has finished speaking chooses the next person.
- The stick may be passed to someone who has not indicated a desire for it as a way to encourage more balanced participation. However, if someone is given the stick and does not wish to speak, she may pass it on to someone else.
- The person with the stick may respond to something that has been said by another or may simply share his experience or idea about the topic.

Processing the Experience

- When the time is up, ring the bell or chime and invite the participants to write quickly what the experience was like for them. If the group is divided into small groups, gather everyone together again to share and listen to each others' responses.
- Pay attention to whether the learnings from using the talking stick have carried over into this time of more informal sharing. Are people listening better and not interrupting? Share with the assembled group what you see.

The talking stick can be used in groups designed for the teaching of prayer. It can also be used in other groups within the church, such as a Bible study, a visioning committee, or a church council. This activity can help to break old habits of debate and discussion and teach people the art of dialogue.

The group sat in startled silence. I could tell they were letting the story touch their hearts. Then slowly and hesitantly they began to respond. "This is a new idea for me," one woman said. "I've long believed that if I finally learned to pray right, my life would become better. Maybe I need to think about the purpose of prayer." Another woman shared that she found the story sad and disheartening. "I want to know that God can fix things," she said. "What you are telling me is that that doesn't happen." "I admire you for continuing to pray," a man said. "I think I would have quit when my life began to fall apart." Many others in the group did not respond verbally, but they had much to reflect on from the story and the responses. No questions were answered, no points were scored, no one was right or wrong. All were engaged in a dialogue about prayer, everyone listened, and hearts were opened to new possibilities. Respect for one another was palpable in the room. This was truly a praying congregation.

FREEDOM TO EXPLORE

Practicing respectful listening and creating safe places to share from the heart gives us the freedom to explore new ways to pray. Discovering and embracing this freedom is part of the process of preparing our hearts for prayer. Do you remember times in your life when you were offered this gift of exploration? One of my early memories is hiking with my family in the High Sierras and my father saying to me, "Run on ahead, Jane. See what's up there." I took off like a flash, set free from my father's slow and steady pace. Later, in high school, I received the freedom to explore in another area. I had an English teacher who assigned us a poetry anthology to read. It was huge and heavy. We all groaned. My teacher's instructions entranced me, though. "Do not read this book from the beginning," he told us. "Skip around, read what you want, find the poems that speak to you for whatever reason. Next week we'll talk about what you discovered." I loved the freedom to start at the back with the more modern poets and I found poems that spoke to my heart. In seminary I took a class from a group called InterPlay.[2] We moved, we danced, we touched, we played. We were freeing our bodies to explore our inner selves, our relationships, the world, and God. I was amazed at the many ways my body could express my feelings. I was thrilled with the wisdom my body contained.

Praying congregations offer their members the freedom to explore prayer in whatever way feels right to them and then provide them with a safe place to share their explorations. I

Creating safe places to share from the heart gives us the freedom to explore new ways to pray.

believe people are just waiting for someone to say, "Run up ahead and tell us what you find," "You don't have to do this in any particular order," or "Let your heart lead you." I also think that many people have claimed the freedom to explore ways to pray that they worry are not acceptable in their church, so they are afraid to tell anyone what they have discovered. Often they have found God in unexpected places or learned a new way to connect more deeply to God. When they hide these experiences and their reflections on what the experiences mean to them, they deny others the richness of their explorations. When I share some of my own experiences in presentations on prayer, participants will often come to me later to say that my stories set them free to share their own.

I will often tell groups how I left the church of my childhood during college, deciding that I was no longer interested in religion, faith, or prayer. My spiritual longings never disappeared, however, and they made themselves known in my early thirties when I went through a difficult and painful divorce. I realized I had no grounding, nothing to hold onto as my life as

ACTIVITY 1.3: SPIRITUAL EXPLORATIONS

Time: At least 45 minutes

Materials: A small table with a simple object on it that represents the life of the spirit, such as a candle, a shell, or a vase of flowers and simple writing materials for each participant.

Setting: Chairs in a circle with the table at the center

Many members of our congregations have discovered God in places other than church. Many of them have had experiences that have deepened and strengthened their relationship with God that they may not have thought of as prayer experiences. This activity is designed to help them think outside a small prayer box and to claim and share a variety of spiritual experiences.

Guided Imagery

- Invite the group to find the most comfortable position for their bodies in the chairs provided or on the floor, if that is appropriate. Ask them to settle themselves and to close their eyes. Help them relax by asking them to follow their breathing in and out, in and out.

- As they relax and you feel they are ready, invite them to look over their lives for times when they felt God was very close, when they knew their relationship with God was growing more intimate. Suggest they look at solitary experiences as well as community activities. Suggest they look in unlikely places (such as a shopping mall or a football game) to explore their relationship with God.

- Give them enough time to remember as many experiences as they are able, and then ask them to focus on one time that seems particularly important or surprising. Help them relive the experience by remembering how their bodies felt, what emotions they experienced, and how their minds were working at the time.

- Ask them to consider whether the experience connected them to the sacred or drew them closer to God. Invite them to reflect on whether they might be willing to name this experience prayer.
- Allow time for silent reflection within the imagery, and then guide them back to the room. Draw their attention to their bodies in the chairs, their feet on the floor, and then tell them that when they are ready, they may open their eyes.

Personal Writing

- Ask the group to remain silent as they write about their memories of this time of exploration.

Sharing

- Break the group into twos or threes to share their experience. Encourage them to share details of how they felt and what they learned. Remind them to consider and discuss whether they would be willing to name their experiences prayer.
- After about 15 minutes of small-group sharing, invite the group back together to discuss what might have become clearer about the breadth and depth of prayer.

I knew it fell apart. I was afraid to return to church, for I believed I would not be accepted. But I knew I needed to find the connection with the sacred that had sustained me in my childhood. In desperation I looked around for help.

I took long, solitary backpacking trips to discover the wonder of creation and feel my connection to the earth. I joined a group of women who formed a drumming circle and rediscovered the freedom and the grounding that comes through rhythm and movement. I read the new books that were being published on women's psychology and began to find affirmation for my journey. I studied Zen Buddhism and began to practice sitting meditation at a local Zen center.

Was I exploring prayer? At first glance it may not seem so, but if you look closely, I think you will see how all these activities led me back to God. During that chaotic period of my life, I was trying to find out who I was and whose I was. I was desperately looking for connection—to the earth, to my own body, to other individuals, and to community. So I started practicing those things that helped me feel connected and grounded. I turned to what was available at that time in my environent—hiking, dancing, reading, and meditating. Slowly I began to realize that I was not alone, that I was connected to the sacred, and that God was present in me and around me. I now realize that my practices were forms of prayer, for they guided me back to an awareness of my relationship with God.

Praying congregations offer their members the freedom to explore prayer in whatever way feels right to them.

A praying congregation does not need to provide these experiences for the people of the church. People can explore new avenues for growth outside the congregation, whether on their own or in small groups. People may go together or alone to a lecture on spirituality for the second half of life. They might attend an interfaith dialogue. Many members of our congregations are involved in twelve-step programs, attend retreats offered by other denominations, take evening courses at the local college or university, and participate in yoga classes. All of these activities can be encouraged and named as part of the spiritual practice of opening the heart. As the members of our congregations venture out, however, we can provide them a place to share what they are discovering. Talking about their experiences will help them articulate how different prayer forms connect them to God and will help others expand their understanding of prayer. Everyone benefits when new experiences of prayer are shared.

Unfortunately, fear of judgment may keep many people from sharing their exciting experiences of self-discovery and spiritual explorations in church. "I never told anyone that I have studied and practiced Buddhist meditation," a woman told me. "I was afraid people would think I wasn't Christian." "I find rich spiritual community in my AA meetings," another man said. "That is where I speak openly and honestly. I just come to church to worship and would never mention that other part of my life." "Our family has been meeting with a Jewish family and a Muslim family who live in our neighborhood," a teenager shared. "We are finding out how we are the same and how we are different. I wish our whole church could know about this."

The willingness to speak about prayer is one marker that a church is becoming a praying congregation.

In a praying congregation where a safe environment has been established, the fears that have kept members from sharing will diminish. They will be able to look back and realize, as I did, that activities they have participated in at different times of their lives have actually been forms of prayer. As they listen to others, they may receive ideas for ways to expand their own prayer lives. These vital conversations are an integral part of a church becoming a

praying congregation. Without them people will pull into themselves and their wisdom and enthusiasm is lost to the church.

BECOMING A PRAYING CONGREGATION

Your church will not become a praying congregation overnight
or even within a year, for developing a prayer ministry is an
ongoing process. Usually the best place to begin is with a small
group of interested and committed people who understand the
church's vital role in teaching people to pray. As this group
gathers to prepare their hearts to learn new spiritual practices,
they can become emissaries to the wider congregation. The
group can support others and give them the courage to talk
about prayer in settings other than "a prayer class." At committee meetings, social functions, or fellowship time, members
of the core group can begin to break the silence and speak
about prayer. Subtle changes will occur as people begin to talk
more openly about prayer. Can you imagine a finance committee beginning with everyone sharing a prayer of gratitude they
had offered that week? What would happen at your coffee hour
if people gently asked each other, "How was your prayer life
this week?" How about a sermon on prayer during which the
pastor shares doubts and confusions as well as assurances? All
of these ideas and many more you can think of will open a
congregation to conversations about prayer.

The willingness to speak about prayer is one marker that a
church is becoming a praying congregation. An experienced
pastor, dedicated to bringing prayer into the individual lives of
church members as well as into the life of the congregation,
told me how little she thought they had accomplished. "I cannot believe it," she said. "A group came to me last week to ask
why we had to share joys and concerns during worship. They
thought it a waste of time and said I should just offer a general
pastoral prayer. I told them how comforting it is to many to

have the issues of their lives lifted up in prayer within the community, but they didn't seem to understand."

The good news about this congregation is that the people were willing to ask and to complain, not only about the music, the seating, or the length of the sermon, but about prayer as well. I know the pastor would have preferred a different approach, but at least they were talking. They were on the journey to becoming a praying congregation.

2

LEARNING TO PRAY

As you begin to explore your own prayer life and if you are called on to guide others in becoming part of a praying congregation, a good place to begin is with how you learned to pray. Those early lessons, whether in childhood or later, are the foundation on which your present prayer life rests. You may not have thought about learning to pray or you may not recall how you were taught or who taught you to pray. But somewhere in your history, someone introduced you to God. Do you know who it was? Do you remember the circumstances such as the place, who else was present, or the words that were said? Maybe you were taught by example as you watched parents or grandparents pray, listened to their words at table grace, or sat with them while they read the Bible. Everyone has a story to tell, even if it is a story about how they cannot remember, or how no one in their early years taught them about prayer. These stories are rich and varied, filled with images and feelings, and make for a lively conversation in a group gathered to prepare their hearts to learn about prayer.

My own memories of learning to pray are filled with contradictions. My parents did not pray at home, or if they did, they did not pray in front of me or tell me that they were praying. They were, however, faithful churchgoers, and I was taken to church at an early age. But my church did not seem to be about prayer. I do not remember receiving instructions on how to pray, but I did receive in church a powerful early image of prayer. Our minister was a large handsome man who had contracted polio as a teenager and who propelled himself around on old wooden crutches. When he prayed during the church service and everyone else's heads were bowed, I watched him stand in the pulpit, his arms outstretched, his face turned upward. He had a look

How did you learn to pray? Who taught you? What were the circumstances?

of such joy on his face that I knew I wanted that experience for myself. The longing for a prayer life came alive for me. But, at the same time, this wonderful man prayed in poetic language, the words rolling out with such resonance and beauty that I thought I could never do what he was doing. I was just a little girl. I did not know all those big words. So at the same time that my desire was stirred, I believed that prayer was beyond me.

Another memory I hold from my early years is attending catechism with my Catholic friend Suzy. In the late 1940s Catholics and Protestants did not mix, but when Suzy told me about going to church in the middle of the week, I wanted to go too. Although my grandmother was horrified, my mother allowed me to go and was interested in what I was learning. I do not remember anything specific, but I do know that I was welcomed warmly by the nuns who taught the classes. I loved going, and I think I got a feeling for what it might be like to live in relationship with God.

I thought that was all I knew about my childhood prayer experiences. Then recently, when my sister and I were talking about our family, she dropped a memory of her own into mine. She is three years older than I, and when we were little we shared a bedroom. She told me that she had always been surprised and a little awed that I would sometimes ask Mother to pray with me at night. She related how Mother would sit on the side of my bed while I told God about friends I was having

Activity 2.1: Memories of Learning to Pray

Time: 30 to 40 minutes

Setting: If this activity is done in a small group, you may wish to place the chairs in a circle. It can also be done with a much larger group where participants are at tables or sitting in pews in the sanctuary.

Memories are often evoked by hearing other people's stories, so this activity begins with the leader telling some memories of how she learned to pray.

Telling Your Story

- Pick two or three vignettes from your experience of learning to pray. They may include both joyful and hurtful memories.
- Tell these stories with as much detail as possible to evoke images in the listener. Use descriptive language, so others begin to feel what your experience was like.

Participants Share

- Say to the group that you imagine that the telling of your story has reminded them of their own memories, and ask them to choose one or two experiences of learning to pray that they would be willing to share with a neighbor.
- After a few moments have them break into groups of three or four, and invite them to share their memories. Encourage them to provide details, so that the others can truly enter into their experience.

Large-Group Discussion

- Bring the group back together, and begin discussion by asking them to raise their hands if they were taught to memorize prayers, then to raise their hands if they were ever told they could talk to God as a friend. Finally, ask them if any of them were taught how to listen to God. These questions and responses help the group see similarities and differences in their experiences.

- Ask if anyone would like to share with the whole group anything particularly interesting or intriguing that they noticed in either their own stories or in the stories they heard. This helps them begin to articulate their understanding of the power of early prayer experiences.

- Invite them to continue this conversation by asking other people in different situations about how they learned to pray.

In every group that I have invited into this dialogue, the participants have responded with eagerness and interest, often hearing new stories from people they have known for a long time. The sharing is also an easy way for a new group to begin to get to know each other.

trouble with, questions that were bothering me, or things I hoped God might give me. I am so grateful for her telling me this story of prayer, for through her memory something I had lost has been found and returned to me. I talked informally to God in those early years. I now realize I have been praying longer than I thought.

Over the years I have heard beautiful stories of children and young people learning about prayer from the adults in their lives. One woman told the story of how every night of her young life, she would run up the cold back stairs to her grandmother's room, climb in bed with her, and snuggle up under a home-made quilt while her Nana recited her prayers in German. "I didn't know what she was saying," she told the group, "but her words seemed full of love, just like her arms around me."

A man said that his parents had taught him the Lord's Prayer and the words to a song that the family sang at meal times. One day at church a Sunday school teacher told him that those prayers were wonderful but then asked whether he knew he could also just talk to God as he talked to his best

> *Remembering your own history of prayer is important as you seek to grow in your prayer life.*

friend. "That made God seem so close and so interested in me and my life," he said. "I still carry on casual conversations with God."

Some memories and stories about learning to pray are not positive. A man told me how he was punished for not getting the words of a memorized prayer right. A woman said that she was told that God would not love her if she did not pray every night on her knees. Another woman shared that her family ridiculed her for believing in God and wanting to communicate with God through prayer.

How did you learn to pray? Who taught you? Do you have warm feelings about the experiences, or do you feel angry or afraid? Remembering your own history of prayer is important as you seek to grow in your prayer life. Some of us were taught to pray as children, others not until later in life. Whenever you received instruction, those earlier experiences are likely to influence how you pray today. Maybe you no longer pray as you were taught; maybe you have found forgiveness and moved beyond some unhappy memories; maybe you wish to reclaim some teaching from an earlier time. Those first experiences of prayer, whenever they occurred, continue to influence the way we pray and the way we teach others to pray.

The Value of Memorized Prayers

Many of us who learned to pray as children memorized prayers and perhaps still recite them ourselves or have taught them to others. When childhood memories are being shared, I am often asked about the wisdom of teaching young children to memorize prayers. My response has not been so much about the prayers themselves or the act of teaching children words they probably do not understand; rather my answer has to do with the vital issue of belonging. Children want to belong to the people they love. They want to be included in the community. When children go to church and all the adults begin to recite the Lord's Prayer, they feel left out if they do not know the words. Once they can join in, they know they are part of this group. They add their young voices to the gathered community. They belong. Since everyone longs for community, teaching our children and other young people the prayers of our traditions is a wise and loving act.

We are apt to see people coming into our churches today who were not taught formal prayers. Like the children discussed above, they often think they do not belong when everyone seems to know words they have never heard. A hospital chaplain told me of planning a funeral for a young couple's stillborn child. The chaplain asked them gently if there was a poem or a scripture passage they would like included in the service. They shook their heads. "What about the Lord's Prayer?" she asked. "What is that?" the young woman asked.

Memorized prayers give us something to hold on to in times of pain, struggle, and grief. When we have no words, the old words comfort us. I was teaching a seminary class on prayer in Denver the day the massacre took place at Columbine High School in Littleton, Colorado. The news reports were not clear, and we had no way of knowing what was actually

> *Memorized prayers give us something to hold on to in times of pain, struggle, and grief.*

happening. We knew only that many lives had been lost and that no one involved would ever be the same. Many students at the seminary had children attending that school. Others knew people who taught there. As we stared at each other in horror, I knew the students were looking to me for guidance. I had no words of comfort, no poetic prayer. I reached out my hand to the student closest to me, and as she took it, all the students joined hands, and together we prayed the Lord's Prayer. I do not know what I would have done if I had been with a group who did not know those wise and familiar words.

Even as we move beyond some of our early teachings to discover a rich and personal adult prayer life, we need to recognize the value of our earlier lessons. As we share our positive memories with one another, we can recognize what words and experiences were helpful to us when we learned to pray. When we hear difficult stories about how others were taught to pray, we can learn what words and methods were hurtful, so that we will avoid repeating those mistakes. Our shared stories can guide us as we teach prayer to the children and adults in our homes and in our congregations.

TEACHING OTHERS TO PRAY

In addition to teaching prayers that can be memorized, we need to affirm the many ways people discover to pray on their own. Children in particular often have a natural instinct to pray, and they offer prayers in a variety of ways. Preverbal children seem to express awe, wonder, and gratitude with their entire beings. As children learn to talk and if they have been introduced to God, they will soon begin to fashion their own prayers. They may tell you that they have secrets with God and ask you to witness their whispered conversation. They may surprise you with a spoken prayer as they sadly bury their pet mouse.

One mother told me how her daughter liked to chant thanksgiving to God for all the beautiful things that she saw as she rode home from school. She confessed that those prayers got a little tiring to her as trees and dogs and yellow cars were all mentioned, sometimes for as long as 10 minutes. "But I didn't tell her to hush," she said. "In fact, I was glad that she had so much to be grateful for." Another mother told me how her four-year-old son climbed up on his chair at dinner one evening as the family began grace. Instead of chastising him, she asked him what he was doing. "I'm standing on my chair," he said, "so that I can be closer to God." A father told me about his two-year-old son, who offered as a dinner prayer one night: "This is the feast of victory for our God! Alleluia!" That proclamation is the beginning of one of the hymns of praise in the Sunday liturgy the family sang regularly. No one had "taught" him the words or suggested they had anything to do with dinner, but he knew!

If we listen to children we will be guided in helpful ways to talk to them, and answer their questions, about prayer.

If we listen to children we will be guided in helpful ways to talk to them, and answer their questions, about prayer. No question about God and prayer should be ridiculed or ignored.

ACTIVITY 2.2: PRAYER QUESTIONS

Time: 30 to 40 minutes

Materials: Writing materials for participants

Setting: Chairs in a circle are preferable but not necessary

Teaching children and others about prayer is most often an informal process and occurs when responding to their questions. At the heart of this form of teaching is listening—so we can discover what the other person really wants to know. This activity is designed to give church members practice in listening carefully and responding honestly to others' questions about prayer.

Discovering the Questions

- Hand out paper and pencil for participants to write down their answers to your questions.
- Ask the following questions, acknowledging that some may not have an answer to one or more of the questions.
    - Write down a question about prayer you remember wanting to ask when you were a child. What prayer questions do you remember having as a teenager?
    - What questions have you been asked about prayer that were difficult to answer?
    - What questions do you have about prayer that you would like to ask now?

Practice Teaching

- Have participants pair with another member of the group.
- Remind them that there is never one correct answer to any prayer question and they are to have fun and explore the many possible ways to answer each question.

- Have them decide who will be first to ask the questions. Invite them to ask their questions one at a time and to listen carefully to the answer offered. They may enter into a brief dialogue before going on to the next question. Remind them that this is not a debate. When one person's questions have all been asked and responded to, the partners will shift roles.
- Invite the partners to share informally what the experience was like.

Discussion

- Bring everyone back together to share what they learned about this informal way of teaching.
- Invite them to think of children or other people that they would like to engage in a discussion about prayer.
- Encourage them to suggest ways they might take their learnings into the congregation.

When children feel safe, respected, and free, they do naturally what we are trying to relearn in our praying congregations—to talk about prayer. And they often go straight to the heart of the matter: "How do I know God hears me?" "I don't think God cares about me; there are too many other important things going on in the world." "If there is no Santa Claus, how do I know there is a God?" "What if I pray for something bad to happen? Will it?" "My friend's sister said that prayer is stupid." Are these not the questions we wrestle with?

Our own wrestling sometimes makes us afraid of children's and other people's questions, for we do not know how to answer them. In our own confusion we often try to avoid the questions, offer pat answers, or give an answer we were taught, even if we no longer believe it to be true. Sometimes we even turn against the person, telling him not to bother us or calling the question or statement unimportant. We are apt to look for any way to avoid admitting that we do not know what to say.

How you were taught to pray as a child can help you become a wise teacher to others.

I am not sure my mother knew what to say when I asked her at the age of nine if Mary, the mother of Jesus, was really a virgin. What I do know is that she took my question seriously and first clarified what I was asking. "Do you know what a virgin is?" she asked. "Yes," I replied. "And you know how babies are made?" "Sort of," I murmured. Wisely, she did not go into a biology lesson. Instead she said, "Well, some people believe she was. Others are not sure. And still others think she wasn't. I think you are going to have to decide what you believe."

Now I really wanted a yes or no answer from my mother. In my young mind Mary was either a virgin or she wasn't! But I suspect that I remember this exchange just because my mother did not tell me what to believe. Instead she told me that my belief was up to me. She let me know in the way she answered that she respected me and had faith that I could sort things out for myself. She turned me toward my own inner knowing and allowed me to make my own choices. She gave no indication that I was supposed to get the answer "right," for right and wrong was not the issue here. Most importantly she let me know that it was safe to ask my questions and wonder about the ways of God.

How you were taught to pray as a child, as well as the stories of how other people learned to pray at any time in their lives, can help you become a wise teacher to others. Remember the delight in some of your lessons, and find ways to share those with your children and others who come to you with questions about prayer. Be mindful of painful experiences, and vow to avoid passing those on. But in addition, as you ponder the best way to teach others to pray, you might be comforted by the wisdom of a 10-year-old who, when asked by his mother who taught him to pray, responded, "Well, Mom, God taught me!"

A Firm Foundation

As you read the stories of other people's memories and as you remember how you first learned to pray, as well as subsequent lessons about prayer, you may wonder if you have a firm foundation for your present and future prayer life. Does your foundation feel a little shaky? Do you wish you had had more exposure to prayer? Do you wonder how your prayer life might be today if you had been taught differently? Do you envy the early prayer experiences of others? An important part of preparing your heart to learn to pray is accepting what you were first taught about prayer and working with it. By remembering, you bring ideas and expectations about prayer out of the shadows and into the light. As you examine your early teachings, you can choose to accept some of what you were taught about prayer and make it part of your spiritual life. You may realize that you need to discard a teaching you no longer find useful. You may also be surprised to discover that an early lesson you thought you had left behind still lingers in your heart.

Hidden in my heart from my childhood experience is the belief that God really does prefer eloquent language to the sometimes incoherent ramblings of my daily prayer. I thought I had rejected that notion, but it still affects me when I am called on to pray out loud. I get nervous as I search for the right

> *By remembering, you bring ideas and expectations about prayer out of the shadows and into the light.*

words, and I am always judgmental of what I have said when the prayer is over.

If you were taught that you needed to pray to appease a judgmental and punishing God, that divine image probably lingers somewhere in your being. Even if you have intellectually discarded that image and have come to believe in a loving, merciful God, there will likely be times when you may wonder if growing closer to God is a good idea. If that happens, you will be quick to resist any form of prayer that offers intimacy with God.

One woman shared how she had been taught as a teenager that she was to go to God in prayer only with love in her heart. She remembered how conflicted she felt when she was angry with her brother or afraid of the kids at school. She wanted to turn to God for help but believed she couldn't go without a loving heart. Until she remembered this early teaching, she wondered why she got anxious when others would talk about expressing anger at God for something that had happened. "You can't do that!" she would say to herself. When her childhood experience became clear, she was able to reevaluate it in the light of her larger image of God. "I shout at God a lot now," she told me.

A praying congregation gives its members an opportunity to do this work of sifting through past experiences to discover what is true for them at this point in their lives. A praying congregation also helps them decide whether their hearts are becoming more ready to explore new ways to pray. When the sorting is done in a community that is safe and respectful, church members are free to discover for themselves what they believe about prayer.

3

WHAT DO YOU BELIEVE ABOUT PRAYER?

Our early experiences of prayer and subsequent teachings about prayer have created in us a set of beliefs about prayer. A praying congregation helps people examine their beliefs about prayer and encourages them to hold on to the ones that are true for them and to discard the ones that no longer fit. When people begin to dialogue about prayer in a safe and respectful community, other people's beliefs will stimulate questions and new ideas. I had this experience while teaching a class on prayer.

A student of mine shared that he believed that all prayer begins with God. This was a totally new idea for me. I had always held the belief that prayer was up to me. I had to initiate the communication; I had to go to God; I had to get God's attention. Considering that God was the initiator of the prayer relationship turned everything upside down. God was already present. God was waiting for me to respond to God's invitation. All I had to do was say yes.

That student's comment was a gift to me. He did not present it as an argument. He was not debating his belief against mine. He simply shared what he believed, and I was free to consider his belief, reflect on it, and decide for myself whether to accept it or not. As I held his comment in my heart, I realized that his understanding of prayer was actually affirmed in my experience.

I do trust God's presence and love for me. I do believe that God is seeking us out. I had just never heard my experience articulated in that particular way. Because of how true this belief felt for me, I decided to let go of my old way of thinking and integrate this new understanding into my beliefs about prayer.

People in a praying congregation do not present their beliefs about prayer as absolute truths that all have to agree with; rather, they engage in dialogue, articulating their beliefs as best they can. As each person offers his or her personal understanding of prayer and others listen carefully, everyone has the opportunity to reflect on their own beliefs. They might ask themselves the following questions:

- Do I agree or disagree with that statement? Is that belief true for me?

- The idea feels true; how can I say it another way?

- What might happen to my prayer life if I integrated that understanding into my belief system?

- Is there another belief that I hold to be true that has not yet been articulated?

- Am I holding a belief that no longer fits? If so, am I willing to let it go?

Examining our beliefs about prayer is exciting and energizing because drawing on our own experiences, listening with our hearts as well as our heads, offers us opportunities to ponder the wonder of prayer. Instead of trying to do this work alone, however, we are wise to reach out to others in our congregation and beyond who are engaged in the search for their own truths. We need to listen to others, hear their wisdom, and allow their experiences to stimulate our minds and hearts. We also need to be in conversation with those who disagree with

ACTIVITY 3.1: BELIEFS ABOUT PRAYER

Time: 45 minutes

Materials: A one-page handout with simple one-sentence statements articulating your beliefs about prayer

Setting: Place the chairs in a circle if the group is small. This activity, however, can be done with any size group in any seating arrangement.

This gathering gives the teacher an opportunity to share with the group what she believes about prayer. Make the list you hand out simple and clear. You may wish to use my beliefs as a starting point, allowing the opening sentences in this section to guide you. However, make the wording your own and be sure you are sharing what you truly believe, so that your group comes to know your experiences and struggles. In your oral presentation, you can expand the simple statements with stories and examples, and respond to questions that arise.

Presenting Your Beliefs

- Remind the group that you are sharing your beliefs, not to convince them that they are true for everyone, but to stimulate their thinking about their own beliefs.
- Reveal your own struggles as well as the strengths of your convictions.

The Group Responds

- Invite the participants to break into groups of three or four. Ask them to respond to what they have heard. What was exciting to think about? What did they disagree with? What belief would they add to their own list?
- Remind them that they are not trying to convince the others in their group that their beliefs are right. They

are to listen for similarities and differences and take the opportunity to reflect on their own beliefs.

Asking Questions of the Leader

- Invite the large group back together to give the participants an opportunity to ask you to clarify any issues they are confused about, share beliefs that you did not address, or disagree with something you said.
- Ask if there are any observations or insights about listening to others' ideas and trying to articulate their own beliefs about prayer.
- Encourage them to continue this dialogue with each other and in their own hearts. Remind them that this is an ongoing process and that clarity will not come in an hour.

This dialogue about prayer must not turn into a debate. The way you respond to the questions that are asked, the opinions that differ from yours, or the discomfort that some may have with your beliefs is the most important part of this activity. As participants share, you might affirm their insights, ask clarifying questions, or paraphrase a statement to make sure you understand. These behaviors, as well as reviewing later what people have said, help participants feel free to disagree with you and others in the group even as they hold on to their own beliefs about prayer.

us as well as those with whom we agree. Different opinions expressed respectfully help us stretch beyond the familiar and into new territory. Such dialogue may be unsettling, for as we examine the way we have been thinking about prayer, we may have to let go of ideas we always believed to be true. When we engage in this stimulating work within our churches, however, we know we are becoming a praying congregation.

Let me share with you my beliefs about prayer to give you a starting place for asking your own reflective questions. Allow these statements to help you discover your own beliefs. Claim your freedom to explore fully what you believe. Agree with me, argue with me, or change my words to fit your experience. Open your heart and mind to the possibility that you do know or you can know what you believe about prayer.

PRIMACY OF PRAYER

I believe that prayer is a primary action. I mean this in two ways. The first way is that prayer needs to be first in our lives, so that prayer guides our actions. We tend to be a people who put prayer last. When everything else fails, we turn to prayer. Rather than prayer being primary, prayer often becomes a last resort. To put prayer first does not mean we necessarily offer verbal prayer before we do anything. Understanding prayer as primary action means that prayer and our grounding in God is the source from which we live. We acknowledge that source with gratitude and thanksgiving.

Another understanding of prayer as primary is expressed by Ann and Barry Ulanov, Jungian analysts and Episcopal priests.[1] Their research and personal faith have led them to believe that infants are born praying. They are so close to God that every sound they utter, from coos to gurgles and whimpers to screams, is prayer. No matter what language infants grow into, their original language is universal. If we believe that prayer is our natural, primary language, then we do not have to learn how to pray. Instead, we have to remember how to pray. For me, remembering is easier than learning something new. I am able to relax and affirm that in my deepest self, I already know how to pray.

RELATIONSHIP WITH GOD

I believe that prayer is all about our relationship with a God who loves us. Prayer is the way we connect and stay connected to God. We enter into this relationship at the urging of God. God wants an ongoing, vibrant, loving relationship with all of us. God desires us not because we are good or holy or set apart in any way; God calls all of us, just as we are, into relationship and offers us the possibility of intimacy. As in human relationships, intimacy grows over time. It does not usually happen immediately, and we progress in our relationship with God as we do with another person.

First, we were introduced to God. Someone may have told us about God by sharing who he thought God to be. Maybe we overheard someone talking about God and asked who that was. Perhaps we have had an experience that made us believe there was something present beyond what we could see or hear or touch and discovered that some people called that something "God." How we were introduced to God will affect the next stages of our relationship with God. If we were introduced to a God of love, we are more likely to pursue a deepening relationship. If we were introduced to a God of anger or to a God who punishes, we may not want to grow closer. We may not wish to sustain the relationship at all.

After we are introduced to God, the next step is to become more acquainted with God. This is when we learn more about who God is and how we feel in God's presence. If the relationship feels comfortable and safe, we may want to become friendlier with God. In a friendly relationship, we are able to relate with pleasure and ease, sharing our thoughts and feelings, asking for advice, growing in trust.

As trust grows we may long to explore the possibility of friendship. We can be friendly with a lot of people, but true friendship takes much more time and a deeper commitment. When we agree to a friendship with God, God becomes a part of our everyday lives. Desire to be with God grows. When in the presence of God, we spend more time listening rather

> *God calls all of us, just as we are, into relationship and offers us the possibility of intimacy.*

than speaking, more time just being together. In friendship we learn to laugh and cry and play together. There is nothing in our lives from which God is excluded as trust grows and the friendship deepens.

Sometimes, intimacy with God becomes possible—not because we deserve it or because we have earned it, but because our longing to be with God is a reflection of God's longing to be with us. When this intimacy happens, we become almost one. We give ourselves over and surrender into the loving presence of God. Often we relish this union with silence, for there are no words to express the joy.

People do not move from introduction to intimacy in an orderly way, and our relationship with God is no more logical than our human relationships. All relationships are messy; they are not linear and cannot be controlled. They unfold and fold back on themselves. There are moments of misunderstanding, separation, and the fear of being abandoned or betrayed. However, if we are committed to the other, we learn to resolve conflicts, reconcile, and trust again. And through it all, love grows. As a relationship with another can move slowly from introduction to intimacy, so, too, our relationship with God can be transformed.

EMBODIED PRAYER

I believe that God wants us to bring all of who we are into this relationship. Nothing is to be left out. God wants our doubts, fears, and anger, as well as our laughter, love, and joy—our greed, envy, and laziness, as well as our generosity, energy, and hope. Think again about human relationships. Love only grows when we are willing to risk being fully ourselves in relationship. If we try to hide our grief or self-doubts, the other misses an important piece of who we are. If we attempt to be the person we believe the other wants us to be, we give up our uniqueness, and the relationship becomes a lie.

In addition to inviting us to bring all of our emotions into our relationship, God wants us to come into relationship fully embodied. It is unbelievable to me that God, who came to us in human form, in a human body, would want us to deny our bodies. We use our bodies to pray as we sing, kneel, and work for justice in the world. We may walk our prayers, dance, swim, or paint our prayers. Our bodies are capable of expressing great love for our creator.

When we bring all of who we are into our relationship with God, we open ourselves to be loved unconditionally.

Our bodies also help us know who God is by experiencing creation with our senses. We know God through the taste of communion bread, in the glory of the sunrise, in the sound of a solitary flute. God comes to us in the sudden rain shower after a long dry spell and in the taste of hot tea offered by a friend. Our bodies help us know that God is as close and as necessary as our every breath.

When we bring all of who we are into our relationship with God, we open ourselves to be loved unconditionally. If we hold back, hide, and pretend to be other than we are, we will never know that the love we feel is unconditional. We might believe that if God really knew who we were, God's love would be withdrawn. This may have happened to us in human relationship. The love we thought was unconditional was in fact dependent on how we looked, behaved, felt, or thought. If we have been wounded by such an experience, it may be hard to trust again. But I believe that God is not only able to love us as we are this moment, but wants to love us in our full humanness.

EVERYTHING A PRAYER

I believe that anything we do that honors, strengthens, or deepens our relationship to God can become a form of prayer. Does this mean that anything we do can become a prayer? Yes, but everything is not automatically a prayer. To fashion our actions into prayers, we need to examine our intention for the activity and God's intention for us. I believe that God intends for us to live according to God's desire that everyone participate in bringing about the reign of God—a world where justice and peace prevail. Therefore, a person swimming as part of her rehabilitation from surgery can turn that action into prayer when she honors God's desire for her wholeness and healing and responds by offering the period of exercise to God.

"Swimming is my deepest form of prayer," a woman recovering from knee surgery once told me. "I imagine I am breathing in God's love and breathing out my worries. And then, because my injured body is so cumbersome on land, I am grateful for how the water holds me up and gives me rest even as I swim. This reminds me how God's love does that for me every moment of every day."

With the intention to honor God, we can make everything we do a prayer if our actions contribute in some way to a just and peaceful world. Doing the laundry for our family, sending a message to a friend, reading a recently published memoir, creating a garden, going to a political meeting, listening to or making music, dancing in the rain—all of these actions can become prayer. Does this seem odd? Does this seem too easy? Shouldn't prayer be more ritualized, more regular? Certainly there are times when we want to offer more formal prayers, and we long for special time set aside to be with God and God alone. But how many hours out of the week do we make time for those forms of prayer? When we broaden our concept of prayer, we are able to be attentive to God during much of our daily activities. I believe that making all we do a form of prayer is what the apostle Paul meant when he told his disciples to pray without ceasing (1 Thess. 5:17). It is also what Brother Lawrence, the seventeenth-century monk who made all his kitchen chores prayer, called "practicing the presence of God."[2]

If you set out to turn all you do into prayer, be gentle with yourself, for if you are like I am, you may find it is more difficult to pray without ceasing than it sounds. I often begin with good intentions, but very quickly my mind wanders, and I have forgotten that I want to deepen my relationship with God through a specific action. I begin to grumble as I fold load after load of laundry. I become frustrated and dispirited at a meeting. I begin to count my worries as I garden. When you notice your attention has shifted, gently bring it back, and know that in your humanness, it will shift again. Sometimes I find that as I forget my intention, God suddenly grabs my attention, and without plan I am back on track. God seems to have a wonderful way of breaking into anything we are doing and reminding us that we are deeply loved.

> With the intention to honor God, we can make everything we do a prayer.

As you reflect on this belief, be aware that how you were taught to pray may influence your acceptance or rejection of this understanding of prayer. If you were taught that the only right way to pray was sitting with your head bowed and your

ACTIVITY 3.2: EVERYTHING A PRAYER

Time: 30 minutes

Material: Writing materials and a talking stick

Setting: Chairs placed in a circle. If the group is large, you may wish to have two or three circles.

This activity is designed to allow participants to explore in more depth what they think and feel about the possibility that everything they do can become a form of prayer. It provides an opportunity to look for places in their own lives where they see some truth in the idea and places where they wonder how it could be true.

Written Reflection

- After people have gathered in their circles, ask them to write brief answers to the following questions:
  — When in your life has something you were doing become a prayer?
  — What activity do you do regularly that you think could become a prayer?
  — Is there any activity you do that you cannot imagine ever being a prayer? If so, what is it?
- Give participants time to reflect and write, assuring them that it is all right if they cannot answer one or two of the questions.

Sharing

- Introduce the model for dialogue using the talking stick. Remind participants of the guidelines outlined in activity 1.2: "The Talking Stick" (see p. 13).
- To begin the dialogue, invite a participant to speak about one of his written answers. The people who follow can respond to what has been said or draw on their own written reflections.

Opportunity to Practice

- When the dialogues are finished, invite participants to share any surprises, insights, or struggles with the whole group, but do not try to summarize or draw conclusions.

- Invite the participants to take their questions and insights into their lives, look for activities that they recognize as prayer, and experiment with ways to make other things they do into prayer. Encourage them to keep a journal.

If this is an ongoing group, begin the next session with participants sharing what they have discovered about the possibility of everything becoming prayer.

hands folded, this idea may seem very strange. If you were taught that God needed certain words from a contrite heart, the possibility of joyfully praying through exercise may push the limits of your belief. Remember that I am not trying to convince you that everything you do can become a prayer. I am simply asking you to reflect on its truth for you.

Prayer and Action

I believe that prayer is not an escape from the world, but rather calls us more fully into the world. The Christian tradition has often divided the things of the spirit from the things of the world, separating contemplation from action. I believe these are false divisions. My experience leads me to understand that prayer and action flow into one another, that they form a circle in which each completes the other. Prayer without action or action without prayer is only half of a faithful life.

As we deepen our personal relationship with God, we strengthen our relationship with all of God's creation. Our prayer does not isolate us; rather, it connects us to sisters and brothers around the world, to the creatures of water, sky, and land, and to the earth itself. As we grow in intimacy with God, we see others and the world as God would see them—with love, mercy, and compassion—and are often moved to acts of charity or social action. Grounded in God we may feel the pain of the earth and become active in eco-justice or simply find a way to conserve water or cleanse our air. When we see what is happening to innocent victims of war, we weep at the destruction of lives and hopes, knowing God weeps with us. Often our weeping moves us to take action—sending money or supplies, attending a peace vigil, or discovering a way locally to act for peace.

> *As we deepen our personal relationship with God, we strengthen our relationship with all of God's creation.*

Similarly, when we act for justice and peace in the world, we realize that our actions must be grounded in God. Without that anchor, we are in danger of thinking that the work all depends on us or that our ends may justify any means. Without prayer support, we are likely to get discouraged and hopeless and turn our backs on a hurting world.

You might think of people you know who are faithful prayers. Are they isolated and uncaring about world issues? They may not be politically active, but are they involved in family and community? Do they tend to the least among us? Does it seem true to you that prayer calls people more compassionately into the life of the world?

A God Who Listens

I believe that God hears our prayers. Trusting that God hears prayers keeps me faithful in prayer. When I experience no answer, I can still keep praying, because I know that God is listening. How or when God answers prayers is unclear to me, and why God seems to answer some prayers and not others is just as puzzling. Someone once said that God answers all prayers with either yes, no, or later. In my experience, that statement is too simplistic, for it ignores the complexities I have witnessed of answered and unanswered prayers.

I trust that people are telling the truth when they relate how they took a question to God in prayer and received an answer. But that has never happened to me. I can look back over my life and see how God has answered prayers and guided me. But I only see the gift in hindsight. I rarely recognize it in the moment.

Sometimes I wonder if I am missing God's response because I am looking in the wrong direction. Maybe God is answering me in a way I do not recognize or understand. During my first marriage, I prayed for a child. I desperately wanted to

ACTIVITY 3.3: ANSWERED AND UNANSWERED PRAYERS

Time: 30 minutes

When people witness to others about their prayer lives, they often tell of the prayers that have been answered. They tell of being healed or an answer received when they were struggling with a decision. These stories are important but so are the experiences of prayers that were not answered. We need to explore the effects unanswered prayers have on our faith.

Remembering

• Invite the group into a period of reflection by allowing them time to settle themselves and quiet their minds and hearts in whatever way is right for them.

• Ask them to remember a time when they believe God answered their prayers. Was the answer immediate or one they recognized later? Do they think it is more accurate to say that God intervened or that God participated in their lives? Allow at least two minutes of silence.

• Ask them to remember a time when their prayers were not answered, some time when they desperately wanted God to intervene and God did not. How long did they continue to pray for help or for answers? How did they feel about the unanswered prayers? What did they think and how did they feel about God?

Sharing

• Divide the group into pairs, allowing people to choose their own partner. If there is an uneven number of participants, allow no more than three together, for this activity often makes people feel vulnerable, and sharing with one other person feels safer.

- Simply invite them to share their experiences of answered and unanswered prayer with each other, encouraging them to listen with open hearts.

General Discussion

- Ask the participants in the large group to reflect on what they noticed and how they felt in the speaking and listening.
- Invite them to reflect on what keeps them praying when their prayers seem to be unanswered.
- Encourage them to begin thinking about how these experiences shape their understanding of God in their lives.

get pregnant. Then my marriage ended, and there was no child. I believed my prayers had not been answered. But 15 years later I married a man with two young sons. Could they be the answer to that long-ago prayer?

I also struggle with the prayers that remain unanswered that I believe a loving God should respond to. A mother's plea for the life of her child. An old man's desire to let go of life and die peacefully. The child's longing for her father to stop abusing her. What happens to our faith when these prayers are not answered? If I depended on the answer I believe God should give to keep me faithful in prayer, I would have stopped praying long ago. But when I trust that God hears those prayers, I am able to keep on praying. If God hears with compassion, then God weeps with the mother, consoles the old man, and rages with the child. God's hearing means God is with us, even if we do not receive the answer we would like.

THE MYSTERY OF PRAYER

I believe that prayer is a mystery. Prayer often surprises us. Just as we think we have figured it out, something new and different emerges. You may be satisfied with your regular morning prayer when all of a sudden you are consistently awakened in the middle of the night with a longing to pray. A different sort of surprise happened to a friend of mine who picked up a book about dancing her prayers, and even as she thought to herself, "I don't dance!" she felt a level of excitement that had been missing from her prayers for a long time.

In prayer we are in relationship with a mysterious God, because God can never be fully known. Made in the image of God, we too are mysterious and never completely known—by ourselves or our closest friends. Some people find the mystery of God and prayer to be disturbing. I find it exhilarating. As I write these words, I realize that it is the mystery that keeps me writing and speaking and teaching about prayer. There is always more to know and experience. I still haven't figured it out. I guess if I had, I would have ended this ministry and moved on to other things.

What do you believe about prayer? Go back to the questions on page 38 and see if you can put together your own list of beliefs. You do not need to defend what you believe. Your ideas may seem illogical and contradictory. The words may not come easily. But clarifying what you believe about prayer will till the soil of your heart and may raise for you some interesting theological questions: "Who is the God to whom I pray?" "Is my image of God the same one I had as a child?" "How do I name God in my prayers?" "Do I trust that God loves me?" These are questions you may wish to explore in a group within your congregation. They are questions that lie at the heart of our growing prayer lives, for as a wise person once said: "The image of God we hold determines how we pray and what we pray for."

4

IMAGES OF GOD

"I think I want to pray, and I keep trying to pray, but something's getting in my way," a student confessed to me. "Every time I try anything but formal verbal prayers, I start getting anxious. When I look at the things that nourish my soul, things I love to do, I get excited, but turning those activities into prayer seems really dangerous. It feels like I'm resisting growing closer to God. Maybe I'm afraid of what becoming intimate with God might mean." Knowing that fear of prayer often indicates confusion about who God is, I asked her what her image of God was, how she might describe God. "Well, I've been taught that God is loving and forgiving, but I'm not sure I really believe it. I look at the suffering in the world and wonder how a loving God could let all this awful stuff happen. Maybe I believe that God doesn't care or that God isn't powerful enough to take care of this mess."

This student's questions and concerns go to the heart of a theology of prayer. Is the God of our understanding and experience a God who welcomes us into relationship and cares about the created world, or do we experience God as remote and judgmental, unable or unwilling to respond to our prayers? Is our image of God one that invites us into intimacy or one that frightens us and makes us wary? Many of us, like the student, can say we believe in a loving and forgiving God. But do we trust that belief, or are there old images of God deep in our bodies and souls that need to be healed before we can truly pray and live from a deep trust in a merciful God?

OLD IMAGES OF GOD

Many of us in the Western world grew up with an image of God as an old, white man with a long beard, sitting on a throne in heaven watching us from above. We may have gotten that image from lessons taught by our parents or Sunday school teachers. Maybe no one said those words but we saw a picture in a book. We could have created that image for ourselves from other words we heard, such as the opening address of the Lord's Prayer: "Our Father, who art in heaven...." Children's imaginations are literal and active. They form pictures from snippets of conversation, ideas they overhear, and longings of their own hearts.

In addition to forming a visual picture of God, many children assign qualities to God, making their images more vivid. These qualities may come from teachings or from their own experience of life. Often these qualities are contradictory and create confusion in a child's mind and heart. A child may be taught that God loves him but then is told not to pray for material things because God has more important things to worry about. For a young child, a small gift is often a token of love, so he feels confused. Another child may believe that God is her best friend and then be told that God will punish her for some mistake she has made. She will likely begin to fear God's judgment.

Most of us have let go of our childhood images of God, but we have not replaced them. We may have some words we say when we are asked to think about who God is but have not spent enough time to reflect carefully and create new images of God. Without some image or images of God that make sense to our minds and touch our hearts, we may become hesitant in

Activity 4.1: Healing Our Image of God

Time: Three or four sessions of 30 to 40 minutes, or two longer sessions if you have the opportunity to extend the class time.

Materials: A copy of *Good Goats: Healing Our Image of God* by Dennis Linn, Sheila Fabricant Linn, and Matthew Linn (Paulist Press, 1994)

Healing our images of God is a long process that involves much of the work we have already done. However, the process of healing is most effective when it includes Scripture study. The best resource that I know of for this process is *Good Goats* by the Linns, which explores biblical images that make people afraid of God as well as passages that proclaim God's love for us. The authors examine biblical passages that tell of God's vengeful punishment and lay them beside passages that proclaim God's unconditional love for us. They discuss as well the idea of hell and issues of suffering and free will using personal and lively stories that engage the reader in the biblical study. The last third of the book includes questions the authors are often asked about the nature of God as portrayed in the Bible and answers they have given. If you are able to provide the participants with their own copies of the book, this lesson can be conducted in the form of a book study. If not, the following suggestions may be helpful in designing your own lessons.

Preparing to Teach

- Read the book, including the section of questions and answers.
- Make note of the points you think are most important.
- Try to think of personal examples to add to the Linns' experiences.

- Decide on the biblical content you wish to include in each session.

Activities to Enhance Learning

- Ask participants to bring to class any biblical passages they find problematic in their search for a positive image of God. Invite them to be prepared to share their personal story about the passage.
- Provide a sample of biblical passages that support a positive image of God. Invite participants to bring their favorite ones to share.
- Ask participants to reflect on what they would need to let go of to heal their image of God, such as their early teachings, an unworthy self-image, fear of failing, or the need to work to earn God's love. Encourage them to explore how the letting go would affect the way they pray.
- Remind the group that you are providing information and a safe place for their reflection and discussion. Your task is not to "fix" anybody's image of God.

our prayers, struggling for words or heaping up empty phrases
(Matt. 6:7). Sometimes we stop praying all together. The longing to pray may not have left us, but since we cannot make
sense of who God is and why we are praying, we simply stop. A
praying congregation can help us discover who God is for us
today. Together we can listen to other
people's stories, express aloud our
confusions and concerns, and wrestle
with a variety of ideas and experiences
to form an image of God and, gradually, a theology of prayer. This dia-
logue will not result in everyone in the community agreeing
on the same theology—that is not the purpose of the conversation. We gather in a praying congregation to talk about our
images of God, for those images will affect how we pray.

*Without an image of God
that makes sense to our minds
and touches our hearts, we
may become hesitant in our
prayers.*

We will find it difficult to explore new ways to pray that
deepen our relationship with God if we do not hold some image of God that calls us to intimacy. It is important to think
through our understanding of God, drawing on Scripture, tradition, and modern theologians. However, thinking, reading
and studying alone will not help us discover an image of God
that is our own, if we do not trust the experience of God we
discover through our prayer. Forming a theology of prayer is
not a linear, rational project, however. It is more holistic and
circular, depending on our experience as well as our thinking
and using our hearts as well as our minds.

NEW IMAGES OF GOD

Think of a time when you felt God's presence. Were you cel-
ebrating a birth? Sitting with friends around a table? Weeping
inconsolably beside your dying mother? Diving into a mountain lake after a long, hard hike? Recalling how you experienced
God during that time may help you form an image of God.

Maybe you felt God's continual wonder at the birth of every child. Maybe you experienced God's presence at that table in the conversation and the breaking of bread. In your sorrow, could you feel God holding you, weeping with you? Was your dive into that lake a metaphor for how you might plunge into the wonder of God? These experiences can guide us toward imagining God as one who loves us unconditionally, weeps with us, comforts us, or delights in us—and make an invitation to intimacy seem possible and perhaps even somewhat difficult to refuse! Tony Hendra, author and comedian, writes of such a God in his book *Father Joe: The Man Who Saved My Soul*. He tells us of Father Joe's experience of God:

> His God was gentle, generous, endlessly creative, musical, artistic, and engineer and architect of genius...who felt ...joy deeply, who could be hurt just as deeply but would never give up on you, who showered you with gifts and opportunities whether you acknowledged them or not, who set you tasks but didn't abandon you if you failed....Father Joe spoke of this person fondly and gratefully, with respect but more than a hint of intimacy....His God might have untold trillions of other concerns, but definitely had time to be Father Joe's best friend.[1]

Such an image warms the soul and invites us into an intimate relationship with God. Who would not want to be this God's best friend? Here is a God to trust, to dance with, and to count on—a God of creativity who nurtures and challenges you to do and be your best but is there to support you when you fall short. Replacing old images of God as a trickster, a scorekeeper, a king, or a puppeteer, with the image of God that Father Joe held dear, is energizing and invites our deepening prayer. When we hold this image of God, we can stop trying to do prayer right. We can let go of the messages that tell us how God wants us to be and simply be who we are in the presence of God. When we heal our negative images of God, we are free to surrender to a loving relationship and participate in the growing intimacy.

Many people find that an image of God such as Father Joe's gives them the confidence to explore new ways to pray. But others may feel the need to think of God as greater and more mysterious than such an anthropomorphic image. "Father Joe's image of God is wonderful," someone might say, "but I think of God as even bigger than that, bigger than a specific being, more pervasive, more everywhere, less 'other.'" These words indicate a search for a God in whom we live and move and have our being (Acts 17:28), a God as close as our very breath, a God who is "in here" as well as "out there."

> *When we heal our negative images of God, we are free to surrender to a loving relationship and participate in the growing intimacy.*

To imagine God out there, in here, and everywhere is to embrace panentheism. This is a fancy theological word that captures the essence of a God who is both with us and beyond us. Panentheism is not to be confused with pantheism, which identifies the universe and all within it as God. The pantheist sees God in the tree and says that the tree is God. Panentheism does not equate everything with God. The panentheist sees God in the tree but knows that the tree is not God; God is more than the tree. In panentheistic thought, God is in you, but you are not God; God is in me, but I am not God. God is more than either of us. Panentheism places God in everything and everything in God. In the words of Marcus Borg, professor of culture and religion: "God is not to be identified with the sum total of things. Rather God is more than everything, even as God is present everywhere. God is all around us and within us, and we are within God."[2]

How might a panentheistic image of God affect our prayer lives? Some people find that a less personal image of God blocks their experience of prayer. "I had a fairly satisfying prayer life," a retired teacher told me, "until I began to read theology. I

Praying with God is simply honoring the presence of God in every aspect of life.

found it fascinating, and it made me think about God in new ways, but I soon realized that I had stopped praying. I was thinking about God rather than relating to God." A young man agreed. "Systematic theology has turned God into an abstraction," he said. "How do you pray to an abstraction?"

Although you may recognize this kind of experience in your own prayer life, I have found that a larger image of God expands rather than diminishes my explorations of prayer. With a larger image of God, I do not need to give up the prayer forms that have nurtured my soul. I still offer adoration and gratitude to a merciful God. I continue to ask God to intercede in my life and the life of the world. I am able to confess my failures to God and receive forgiveness. But the God of these prayers is only one aspect of a much larger and more mysterious God who is not only "out there" but "in here," who is ultimately not separate but is one with everything. Being already one with God provides me the option of praying *with* God as well as *to* God.

To pray with God is not to ask anything of God or to tell God everything. Praying with God is simply honoring the presence of God in every aspect of my life. I pray with God, and God prays with me. I pray in God, and God prays in me. We are one, and we honor that reality. I pray with God when I dance with joy, when I weep in despair, and when I speak out for justice. I pray in God when I sit, silently gazing out the window at winter's first snowfall, enveloped in the silence of creation. God prays in me when I feel a longing to be still in the presence of God, when I am moved to reach out to someone in need, or when I am filled with love that I cannot keep

ACTIVITY 4.2: GOD IS EVERYWHERE

Time: 45 minutes

Materials: Crayons, colored markers, or other drawing tools, and a piece of chart paper for each participant

Setting: Chairs at tables so that participants have enough room and a hard surface on which to draw

When children and adults are asked to draw their image of God, their drawings often include something human, such as hands, a smile, or a lap to sit in. Sometimes the image is of a complete person sharing love, judgment, anger, or joy. The purpose of this activity is to invite group members to explore concepts of God beyond these anthropomorphic images.

Preparation for Drawing

- Put paper and art supplies on every table, and invite the participants to find a space.
- Reassure them that this activity has nothing to do with their ability to draw; rather, that we use art materials and images to help us know God in ways our linear minds cannot.
- Suggest that if they feel uncomfortable anticipating putting anything on paper, they can draw with their nondominant hand. This gives them an excuse for the picture not looking "good."

Guided Reflection

- Invite the participants to relax and center themselves by closing their eyes and paying attention to their bodies, then their feelings, and finally their thoughts. Give them plenty of time and silence before you begin the reflection.

- Invite them to imagine God as everywhere. You might use the words I use on page 61 such as "all around," "within," "more," "out there," and "beyond." Say these words slowly, add others, repeat some of them to provide a litany to surround them.
- Ask how it feels to imagine God this way. Invite them to remember times when they experienced God everywhere. Then slowly repeat the words of the litany.
- After a few minutes of silence, say: "When you are ready, you may open your eyes and begin to draw. Try not to plan what you will draw; simply pick up a color and begin. Let the colors and the shapes guide you. Please remain in silence as the drawing continues."

Sharing

- When most people are finished, you might ask them to gaze at their drawings and see what the drawing tells them. They may want to write something on the drawing about their experience of creating this image of God.
- Invite them into pairs to share their drawings. Remind them not to analyze or criticize each other's drawings in any way. They are to listen with their hearts as well as their minds and see what their drawings have to teach them.
- Conclude the activity by gathering everyone into a group to share what the experience was like and what they have learned about new images of God.

from overflowing into the world. Praying with God is simply about presence—my presence in God and God's presence in me. Imagining God in the midst of life makes the practice of presence possible and brings with it a quiet assurance of my oneness with God.

CONSIDERING GOD'S POWER

We might feel pleasure and comfort as we explore a panentheistic image of God. However, this image may call into question many of our beliefs about the power of God. If we imagine God as entirely other from ourselves and creation, and if we attribute power to this God, then God has power over us and the world. We may have some power but always less power than God. If we hold a negative image of God, we see God's power used to judge, punish, or seek revenge. Holding a more positive image of God, we will see God's power being used to create justice and peace and goodwill among people and nations. Whether the images are negative or positive, both indicate that God has power over us, our actions, and the fate of the world. This image of an all-powerful God is common in our Christian tradition.

To imagine God inside as well as outside creation calls us to a new understanding of God's power. In panentheistic thought, God's power is as absolute as in other images, but in this thought, God's power is understood to empower rather than to control humankind. God's power becomes a force that is used with us and for us, rather than a force held over us. The divine power empowers us to speak, act, and live in accord with God's covenant with God's people. We are called to speak and act for peace and justice, live with kindness and forgiveness, and treat our neighbor as ourselves. We are radically dependent on God's loving power to help us live this way, and God is radically dependent on us to create the world we have been promised. Understanding God's power as empowerment calls us into an interdependent relationship with God.

Interdependence in a human relationship means that I depend on the other person just as he or she depends on me. So it is in our relationship with God. I depend on God and God depends on me and empowers me to contribute to the building of God's reign on earth. In other words, we need God and God needs us. When I spoke those words in a Sunday school class years ago, a woman shouted out from the back of the room: "I hate that idea! I don't want to believe that God needs me. Everyone in my world seems to need me right now. To think that God also needs me is just too much!"

> *I depend on God and God depends on me and empowers me to contribute to the building of God's reign on earth.*

The class was silent for a moment after her outburst and then broke into a lively discussion. Class members shared their experiences of times when they were dependent on God and other times when they realized God was dependent on them. "When my sister was killed in a random mugging, I could do nothing but cling to God," a man told us. "I was numb and paralyzed and unable to think or act rationally for weeks." "I know that experience," another man said. "But when I think of the time I confronted some teenagers bullying a disabled man, I understand God's need for me. God's need for all of us." As others shared their experiences of radical dependence on God and times when God depended on them, many class members began to understand that God's need for them did not preclude their sometimes desperate need for God's loving presence in their lives. They were able to embrace both realities: their dependence on God and God's dependence on them.

The woman who had started this discussion with her outburst said that after listening to others' thoughts, she felt better than she had when she had first spoken, and was able to contribute valuable insight to the discussion of interdependence. She said she thought that interdependence was not a static experience but was a relationship that shifted, depending on the circumstances of one's life. "Right now, I feel overwhelmed," she shared. "I think I need God more than God needs me. Or maybe I am simply unable to hear and respond to God's needs at this time. But later, as I get stronger, I may be able to become more interdependent with God." The group was quiet while they pondered this, and then another intriguing issue was raised: "If God is not all powerful in the old way of thinking, how do we pray for God's intervention in our lives and in the world?"

DIVINE INTENTION AND DIVINE INTERACTION

Prayers of petition and intercession are among the most common prayer forms in the Christian tradition. In both of these prayers, we are asking God for something. We may be expressing our desire for something specific in our own life, such as a job or a new friend. Sometimes we ask God for specific qualities, such as patience, courage, or wisdom. In our intercessory prayers, we may ask God to intervene to help resolve a personal or community conflict, bring peace to a war-torn country, cause rain to fall on the parched earth, or heal an injured love one. All these prayers indicate our desire to have God change or fix what we experience as wrong in our lives and in the world. However, if we imagine God as one who empowers rather than one who wields power over external events, prayers of petition and intercession may seem useless. For if God is not going to use divine power to intervene in our lives and respond to our requests, what is the purpose of these forms of prayer?

Divine intervention is a powerful concept and one that we may cling to. How comforting to believe that God could intervene in our lives at any moment and make everything right. But that belief is not congruent with panentheistic thought, for God is not "out there" waiting to be called upon to take action. God is here, present, with us—always and everywhere, already participating in our lives.

Participation is different from intervention. If we are willing to give up our reliance on divine intervention in favor of God's participation, we can discover the power of divine intention and divine interaction.[3] Divine intention is God's promise through Scripture and tradition that all of creation is good and that we are meant to live in harmony with one another. God's vision and promise for each of us is not an easy and painless life, but God's intention is for healing and wholeness in the midst of our struggles. God interacts with us, supporting and encouraging us, to bring about that intention, to bring harmony and wholeness into our lives and the life of the world. Divine interaction gives us the opportunity to choose to cooperate with God.

If you embrace a theology that understands God to be with us as well as beyond us, an empowering God rather than an all-powerful God, you may have to let go of the idea of divine intervention, the notion that God can reach from beyond to take care of anything that

Divine intervention is a powerful concept and one that we may cling to.

is wrong. This change may feel like a great loss if you have counted on God to fix your problems, repair your mistakes, and heal the pain and brokenness in your life and the life of the world. On the other hand, trusting in God's intention and willingness to interact with us empowers us to act and gives us hope—hope that is different from the hope we might have felt when we prayed with the expectation that God would make the wrong things right. Through this model I can understand my responsibility in my own healing and the healing of the world. But I also recognize this healing is not all up to me, for others are praying and working to fulfill God's promise, and God is also present, interacting with us all. With this understanding we create a new image of God and the nature of our relationship with God, as well as the way God responds to prayer.

When we embrace this image of God and God's power, we may offer prayers of intercession and petition in the same way we have prayed before. Those familiar prayers connect us to the love of God that is always present, give us comfort in times of struggle, and remind us we are not alone. We do not *We pray knowing that we are radically dependent on God even as we are recognize our own responsibility.* need to stop our heartfelt prayers for the healing of a loved one or peace in the world. But rather than praying these prayers with the expectation that God will respond by fixing what is broken, we pray knowing that God may help us attend to ways we might assume more responsibility. We pray trusting in God's healing intention for us and the whole creation, and God's interaction in our lives and the life of the world. God interacts with us through other people, friends, or strangers who offer us help or support in times of need. God also often interacts with us through the written word. We can find God's wisdom, not only in Scripture, but in poetry and novels as well. We may find hints of the divine in nonfiction such as a recent issue of a scientific magazine, or an article or book on economics. We interact with God, too, when we pay attention to the wonders of nature and reach out to others in love and forgiveness. God calls us to trust the divine intention and divine interaction in all aspects of our lives. As we develop that trust, we pray with the knowledge of God's closeness and availability. We pray knowing that we are radically dependent on God even as we recognize our own responsibility. We pray to, with, and in a God who is present.

The presence of God and the prayers of my friends sustained me last year when I was hospitalized with a serious case of West Nile Virus. There is no cure for the virus, and it can cause great damage to the body as the immune system tries to figure out how to fight the infection. As I lay in bed with a high fever and in terrible pain, I knew I was being prayed for. Friends from many parts of my life had been notified of my condition, and prayers were being offered for my recovery. I did not expect those prayers to cause God to heal me. What I did know and trust was that God's intention was for healing and wholeness and that God was interacting with me and all those who were participating in my care.

I was released from the hospital after six days with the effects of menengio encephalitis, which is a swelling of the brain and spinal chord. Full recovery took seven months, and during that time I continued to be sustained by prayer—my own and others'.

In the same period many people died as a result of the virus. Did God cure me and not others? Were the prayers of my community more effective than the prayers offered by other communities? I might have to think so if I believed in divine intervention, for if God was called on to heal all who had contracted the virus, my recovery must mean God chose to heal me and allowed others to die. Because of my understanding of God's power as empowerment, however, I do not feel singled out in any special way. I simply trust that God's intention was the same for us all, and I believe that God interacted with all patients and caregivers for that intended healing and wholeness. Some of us lived and some of us died, and God was present with us all. That is the mystery of God and of prayer.

The mystery is what sustained me then and sustains me now. I do not understand why I lived and recovered fully while others who lived still suffer from permanent disability. But I

ACTIVITY 4.3: DIVINE INTENTION AND DIVINE INTERACTION

Time: 30 to 40 minutes

Materials: Paper and pencil for each participant

Setting: Chairs in a circle if the group is small, but this activity can be done in a larger group with participants seated at tables or in rows

Most people think of divine intervention when they participate in intercessory prayer. This exercise is designed to help members of your group think in a different way about intercessory prayer and God's response to those prayers.

Remembering a Time of Prayer

- Ask participants to remember times when they were involved in intercessory prayer. These could be experiences of praying for another or of receiving prayers. Invite them to choose one of those experiences to focus on. Encourage them to choose one that was powerful and elicits deep feelings.

- Invite them to close their eyes and remember that experience with as much detail as possible.

Asking Reflective Questions

- Tell the group that you are going to ask them three questions. Following each question, participants are to open their eyes and write down a brief answer, and then close their eyes again and return to remembering their experience of intercessory prayer.

- Question 1: Did you experience God intervening in your life or in the life of the one you were praying for? How did you know it was divine intervention?

- Question 2: Did you sense that God held an intention—a promise—in the situation that you or others were praying for? What was that intention?

- Question 3: Can you see how God interacted with you and others in the particular experience you are thinking of? Who did God interact with, and what form did that interaction take?

Sharing

- Invite participants to share in small groups the prayer experience and any part of their answers that particularly interests them.
- After all participants have shared, have them stay in the same group to discuss the following question: How might these concepts of divine intervention, intention, and interaction enliven or change in any other way their prayers of intercession? What problems do they see?
- Conclude the session with a brief period of large group exploration and sharing.

know that God was present in my hospital room. God was interacting with my physicians and nurses, with my family and friends who stayed by my side. God was interacting with me as I did the hard work of physical therapy and was present in the long periods of rest that would facilitate my healing. God did not intervene

> *God is multifaceted and mysterious, beyond even our wildest dreams.*

to heal me, but God was with me, filling me and surrounding me with love. Prayers in many forms from many people helped me remember the power of God's presence in all our lives.

As you sort through your images of God—remembering old ones and exploring new ones—be gentle with yourself. You may not know for a while what you believe. You may find that a number of images of God feel true. Remember that there is no right answer or even one answer to the wondrous question of who God is. You do not need to decide on one image to the exclusion of others. God is multifaceted and mysterious, beyond even our wildest dreams. Draw on all the images of God that make sense to your mind, heart, and experience. The image of God you hold will determine how you pray and what you pray for. As you seek to grow in prayer and your relationship with God, however, practice praying with those images that invite intimacy, give comfort, challenge you to new ways of prayer, and encourage you to pray without ceasing.

5

PRAYING ALL WAYS AND ALWAYS

"I want to be praying more, but I just can't find the time," people often tell me. "I set aside intentional prayer time, but I get interrupted," others will say. Those seeking a deeper relationship with God often desire to spend more time in prayer. You may feel that same longing, but before you try to devote more time to prayer, I suggest you examine all the ways you are praying now. Many of us pray more than we realize. The only way to learn new ways to pray is to broaden our understanding of prayer and discover how many forms of prayer are already present in our lives. When individuals within a community begin to claim their identity as pray-ers, the church is more able to become a praying congregation.

RENEWING YOUR SPIRIT

One way to discover what is already an integral part of your life of prayer is to ask yourself what you do, even if not very often, to renew your spirit and nurture your soul. Another way to ask the question might be: "What helps you connect to the presence of God?" You can explore these questions alone, but it is more fun and fruitful to do it in a group, for people's experiences trigger other people's ideas. I have asked this question in classes, and we have covered the board with many diverse and sometimes amusing ways people replenish their spirits. Groups often begin with such things as Bible study, Sunday worship, being in nature, listening to music, journal writing, and playing with their grandchildren. But when encouraged they can expand their lists to include reading mysteries, taking bubble baths, watching cartoons, washing the dog, napping, and making love.

While sharing ideas in a group, pay attention to when you become judgmental. It is common for people to think during

> *What do you do to renew your spirit and nurture your soul? What helps you connect to the presence of God?*

this activity: "How in the world does that nurture his spirit?" or "What is she thinking by saying that connects her to God?" If you are aware of your thoughts and feelings, you may receive clues about activities you have decided have no place in your spiritual life. Maybe you are not willing to accept those things that are simply fun as nurturing to your spirit. Maybe you have ignored the sensual in your understanding of ways to grow closer to God. Maybe you never thought of including anything other than Scripture or devotional material as spiritual reading. You need not agree with or adopt anyone else's ideas about how to nurture your own spirit, but if you are open, someone else may point you in a direction you had never imagined.

After sharing ideas and completing their lists, group participants often tell me that if in this activity I had said, "Name all the ways you pray," instead of asking them to share what nurtured their spirits, they would never have come up with so many ideas. Because I asked a broader question, they were able to see that the ways they nurtured their spirits could in fact be forms of prayer. They had to think outside their narrow understanding of prayer to realize all the ways they prayed. As we discussed in chapter 3, all these activities are not automatically prayer, but because they are ways that people naturally connect

ACTIVITY 5.1: RENEWING YOUR SPIRIT

Time: 30 minutes

Materials: Large white board or pieces of chart paper that can be displayed and paper and pencil for each person

Setting: Chairs arranged in semicircles or rows, facing the board

Approach this activity playfully and in the spirit of fun. The task is to have participants name all the things they do that nurture their spirit. When the group thinks they have completed the list, encourage them to find more, to look into ignored areas, and to remember what they did as children. Add your own ideas, and be accepting of everything that is offered.

Asking the Question

- Ask, "What do you do that renews your spirit?" "What do you know that nurtures your soul but you do not do or haven't done in a long time?"
- Record responses on the white board or on newsprint.

Reflection

- Using the collective list, invite participants to make a personal list of the things that nurture their spirit that they do or have done, as well as things on the group's list they would like to do. Tell them that they will not be asked to share their lists with others and that they may want to add other activities that they wish to keep private.
- Ask participants if they would be willing to call these activities "prayer."

Sharing

- Allow time for the group to share any insights they have gained from the experience without sharing the items on their lists.

to God, the practices can easily become prayer. With the intention to honor God in all we do, the activities listed become the means to practice the presence of God.

PRACTICING THE PRESENCE OF GOD

You might pick one of the activities that nurtures your spirit and think for a moment how you might make it a prayer. What about reading mysteries is prayerful? Is it your concern for the battle between good and evil? Might it be the joy of not knowing what is going to happen or the willingness to be surprised? Could the full attention we give the story be a metaphor for the way we might attend to God? If any of these ideas connect your reading to prayer, simply focus your attention on the connection the next time you sit down to read. Be aware of how reading the story honors your relationship with God.

One way to practice the presence of God is to make a morning intention to open your heart to God's guidance throughout the day.

A friend of mine in her seventies shared how the classes she attends in line dancing have become a prayer for her. She believes that God wants her to take good care of her body, and this form of exercise is one way she does this. She also trusts that God wants her to express her joy and delight. She loves to dance and does so with great enthusiasm. In addition, she finds that learning the steps and moving together with others is a reminder of the way we are called to be in relationship with our brothers and sisters. "And sometimes," she exclaimed, "I feel like I am dancing with God."

Another way to practice the presence of God is to make a morning intention to open your heart to God's guidance throughout the day. You might want to create your own intention or take guidance from other people's prayers. One man's morning prayer sounds like this:

Gracious God, I thank you for the gift of this new day. Let each of my activities and my encounters with others reflect the love I have for you. Help me be open to your guidance as I move gently through my day. Remind me of your constant presence and your love for me, so that I will know I do not walk alone.

One woman shared that she begins her days with these words:

Good morning, Lord! Thank you for another day! Thank you for my health, my family, my life! What are we going to do today? What new person, new idea, new project are we going to encounter today? How can I make this day even better than yesterday? Let's go, Lord! I'm ready!

I like to make my morning intention without words. I stand and stretch my arms up high indicating my awareness of the wonder of the presence of God in my life. Then I reach in front with my hands cupped, showing my willingness to receive the gifts of the day. Next, I bring my hands together over my heart to remind myself that I must fully take in those gifts before I am ready to share them. To demonstrate the act of giving, I swing my arms and hands at waist level, back and forth, as if to scatter my gifts. I end with my hands pressed palm to palm at my heart level and bow my head to enact receiving the blessing of God. I often do this three times, sometimes lingering longer in some positions than others, depending on the needs of that particular day.

Knowing that we are apt to forget our intentions, many people select some sort of reminder during their day to refocus their attention on God. In the monastic life, monks and nuns are called to times of regular daily prayer. When it is time for community prayer—or the liturgy of the hours, as it is sometimes called—they stop whatever they are doing and join their sisters or brothers in prayer. In some Buddhist communities, a bell is rung at irregular times during the day, calling all to be mindful of the present moment.

Those of us outside monastic communities could use a similar reminder. We might set a chime on our watches, not so we will know what time it is, but as a way to recall our prayerful intention and turn our attention to God. A woman who spends much of her time in the car allows red lights to serve as her reminder. Instead of waiting impatiently for the light to change, she turns her heart and her mind to God. Another person says that police and fire sirens are his call to attention. Whenever he hears that clamor, he offers prayers of intercession for all those involved and he remembers that God is with us, even in the struggles. All of these practices serve as a guide to prayerful living and begin to create what some would call a rule of life.

A RULE OF LIFE

Benedict of Nursia, a sixth-century hermit, became the author of one of the early rules used by Christian communities. The rule was written to articulate right relationship among those who had gathered to live in the presence of one another and to devote themselves to God. Although Benedict had gone off by himself to be alone in prayer, serious seekers were attracted to his devout ways and joined him in his search for a deeper relationship with God. To guide the growing community that surrounded him, Benedict wrote his rule in which balance was a core value. He recommended times of solitude and community, work and rest, study and recreation, corporate worship and prayer alone.[1] This corporate rule guides many monastic communities today and is often used by individuals to guide their spiritual lives.

If you try to imagine an individual "rule of life," you might imagine such a rule would be rigid, confining, and difficult to adhere to. You might think it is something that others who are more holy have designed and dutifully follow. I like to imagine the rule as a trellis guiding our growth and giving

ACTIVITY 5.2: DAILY INTENTIONS

Time: Allow at least 10 minutes to explain this activity as a homework assignment.

This activity is best done at home during the week. Invite the participants to linger in bed each morning and take time to reflect on how they might practice the presence of God that day.

Encourage them to create a prayer of intention for the day ahead and to write the prayer in their journals. If the intention does not include words but is expressed through movement, music, or images, invite them to make a few notes for themselves and for sharing later.

Encourage them to create a different intention each day, so that they have a number of options from which to choose as a regular intention practice for the weeks and months to come.

At the next group meeting, invite members to share their discoveries and their decisions, helping them attend to the process as well as to the outcome.

us something to hold onto. Just as a climbing plant needs something to support it, we need the same assistance. We already have some structure in our lives whether we are aware of it or not. Recall things you do regularly and rarely miss. Do you eat dinner every night at six? Watch the news daily? Do you work in your yard on a regular basis? Is your grocery shopping done on the same day every week? Do you have a club or group you meet with weekly or monthly? Do you attend church almost every Sunday? All these activities are guidelines that give form and structure to your days. When you do not do them for one reason or another, your life may begin to feel chaotic. Even if some activities and commitments occasionally feel like obligations, you may miss not doing them.

> *Be honest with yourself as you try to discover the rule of life you live by—you may want to shift your intention, so more of your rule attends to God.*

To examine the rule of life that is guiding your spiritual formation and your prayer life, return to the list you made in activity 5.1: "Renewing Your Spirit" of things you do that nurture your relationship with God. See what activities you do daily, weekly, monthly, or yearly. The spiritual practices that you do regularly constitute your rule of life. Then ask yourself with what intention you do these things. Do you do them primarily as a spiritual discipline, to meet your family expectations, or maybe because your doctor strongly suggested them? Whatever the intention, these activities are part of your rule. You may want to consider shifting your intention, so more of your rule attends to God. Be honest with yourself as you try to discover the rule of life you live by.

As you become more aware of what guides your life you can consider making changes you think would be wise and helpful. Begin by asking yourself if there are activities that you would like to add, or maybe do more often, or for a longer period of time. You might want to add some solitude time to your weekly schedule, or if you live alone, you may recognize the desire to find more time to be with others or in community. If you already walk twice a week, would it be a good idea to walk three times a week? Maybe you spend 20 minutes in the morning in intercessory and silent prayer. Would you like to increase that to 30 minutes?

As you lightly and prayerfully hold this emerging design—or rule—let yourself be guided by these three questions posed by retreat leader and author Marjorie Thompson in her book *Soul Feast: An Invitation to the Christian Spiritual Life:*

- What am I deeply attracted to, and why?
- Where do I feel God is calling me to stretch and grow?
- What kind of balance do I need in my life?[2]

The first question is to guard against your designing a rule of life you think you *should* be following rather than a rule you *long* to follow. You may try to create a rule based on your idea of how prayerful people should behave. You might know someone who has been following a rule of life with great joy and want what that person has. We can learn from listening to other peoples' rules, but if we do not put into our rule those things that we deeply and truly desire, we often abandon our rule soon after we have begun.

I was once tempted to make that mistake when I heard someone I respected describe his rule of life. His rule consisted of the following practices: Every day he ran for 45 minutes. After his shower, he spent half an hour in Bible reading and silent meditation. Each evening before he went to bed, he spent 15 to 20 minutes in an examination of conscience. Once a week for a half day, he found a way to be alone in nature, and every month he spent a full day at a nearby monastery. He loved his rule and was energized and inspired by following it. His attitude toward life and others was loving and kind. People were drawn to his quiet humor and the passion he had for God and life.

As I listened to him talk I began to feel awful. My rule looked nothing like his, and his seemed much holier than mine. I wondered how I could add some of his activities to my day. I tried to imagine myself following his rule—and I couldn't. I felt guilty and sad. I was not listening to my own heart for what I truly desired. I was trapped in trying to be like someone else. I know he did not share his rule to make anyone feel bad or "less than." He simply wanted us to know what joy can be found in a rule of life and how many ways we can intentionally draw closer to God. When I realized what I was doing, I returned to my own rule and the desires of my own heart.

> *Guard against designing a rule of life you think you should* be following *rather than a rule you* long *to follow.*

The second question, "Where do I feel God is calling me to stretch and grow?" helps keep us from getting too complacent. Although it may not be wise to listen to someone else's needs and longings to see what changes to make in our own rule, it is wise to listen to God. Is God calling you to take a risk and try something new? Is God inviting you to look at new ways to deepen your relationship with God and all of creation? Look at those activities and practices you seem to have been avoiding yet are interested in trying. Maybe God is calling you into something new. Be willing to try the new activity for a short period of time. Just because you begin does not mean you are stuck forever with a new practice. If you discover that it really does not help you become more intimate with God, you can let it go. You might discover that you love a new practice but that it does not fit in with the other responsibilities and commitments in your life. You can set it aside, perhaps for another time in your life.

Activity 5.3: Your Own Rule of Life

Time: 45 minutes

Materials: The list of activities from activity 5.1: "Renewing Your Spirit" that was done by the community, each person's individual list, and more writing material

Setting: Chairs placed to make individual reflection possible

You can combine this activity with activity 5.1: "Renewing Your Spirit," completing both at the same group session if you have time, or giving part of this activity as homework.

Examining the Rule

- Invite the group to pay attention to the activities they do regularly to guide their spiritual formation. Regularly may mean daily, three times a week, weekly, monthly, seasonally, or yearly.
- Ask participants to circle those activities they want to keep as part of their rule, check the ones they would like to do more often, and scratch through the ones they believe are no longer useful.
- Invite them to make another list of those things they are not doing that they would like to add.

Developing a New Rule

- Review Marjorie Thompson's three questions with the group, and ask participants to use them to reflect on all the practices they have written down, circled, scratched out, or checked.
- Provide 15 to 20 minutes of quiet time for participants to work on their own rule.
- Ask them to put their tentative rule in some form that they can share with another.

Sharing Their Rule

- Ask the group to gather in threes or fours for sharing.
- One person will begin by telling the others what his rule looks like. The others listen to discern whether the rule is balanced and fits the person's desires and whether he has listened to God's prompting.
- After the rule has been shared, the others can ask clarifying questions such as: "Is that realistic?" "Do you really want to do that?" "Is there something that stretches you into new areas?" "Do you think you have enough time in community to balance your solitude?" These questions need not be answered. They are asked as ways to help the other think more deeply about his or her rule of life.
- Each person takes a turn to share and receive feedback. The leader may need to keep track of time and give the groups a signal when they are to change roles.

Living the Rule

- Invite the participants to begin living their rule the next day.
- Tell them to pay attention to their desires, any resistance that may appear, or their inability to follow their rules. Remind them to be gentle with themselves, that developing a rule is an ongoing process.
- Let them know that they will have a chance to share their experience with their rule the next time they gather.

A young woman who was introduced to the method of centering prayer found it to be a natural prayer form for her. She slipped into it with ease and found it nourishing and enriching. She had never before found a way to be silent with God. She went to classes and retreats to pray with others when she could. However, she was unable to practice centering prayer regularly at home, no matter how hard she tried.

She made an appointment with one of the teachers at the retreat center to talk about her love for the prayer and her discouragement at not being able to adhere to a daily practice. The teacher listened to her story and then asked: "What is your life like at home right now?" "Oh," she said, "I have three children under six, I work part-time, and my husband travels a lot. Plus I am an active volunteer in my church." The teacher replied to her gently, "My dear, come and pray with us as often as you can, but don't worry about not practicing at home. In your situation, I think your daily prayer should

Where do I feel God is calling me to stretch and grow?

simply be 'help' and 'thank you.' Let go of trying to do what is impossible. Clearly this is not the right time to try to find silence at home."

Marjorie Thompson's last question invites us to examine our rule of life for balance. Do you always depend on your faith community for prayer, or do you have solitary prayer practices? If you are a student, do you make time for recreation and activities outside your field of study? Do you know how to find rest on a regular basis, or do you rest only when you are ill? Are you able to be alone with yourself, or do you flee solitude?

When you find imbalance, go back to the first two questions, and see if you have a strong desire for something that would help you find balance. Then listen to God to discover what changes might be in order. Remember that balance is a dynamic term. No one achieves permanent balance in life. All we can do is notice when we are out of balance and gently take steps to correct the imbalance. Then we wait until we slide out of balance once again, pay attention to where we are, and shift to make the correction.

I find the image of a moving sailboat helps me recognize how maintaining balance is an ongoing process. A sailboat does not steer a direct course to its destination. Depending on the wind, the sailor needs to tack back and forth to stay on track. We are like the sailor, attending to where we are and where we are going, making subtle corrections as we sail along. In this ongoing process of correction, we find balance in our rule of life.

Accountability

Being accountable may make you think that someone will be checking up on you, watching to see if you falter or fail. But being accountable for your rule of life and the ways you pray means knowing that you have somewhere to go where you can talk about prayer. All of us need a place to stop and reflect with another listening heart, and report how our prayer lives are going. We need to share what we have discovered about new ways to pray and how we feel about practicing those methods faithfully. We have to find a place where we can get new ideas when we get stuck. We particularly need a place to go when we get discouraged and realize that we have not lived up to our own expectations. A praying congregation can provide such a place. Members of such a congregation will be eager to listen to your stories and sometimes may not wait for you to come to them. They might call to find out how you are and ask you simple and profound questions such as: "How goes it with your soul?" "What is happening in your prayer life?"

These are the questions spiritual friends ask each other. A spiritual friend, sometimes called a soul friend, is someone willing to listen to your thoughts and feelings about all aspects of your relationship with God. You in turn will be willing to provide this same deep listening for your friend. You may already have people in your life with whom you share deeply, but an intentional soul friend may become important to you as you till the soil of your heart and discover new longings to pray.

All of us need a place to stop and reflect with another listening heart about how our prayer lives are going.

Having a spiritual friend is not the same as going to a spiritual director. The content of the relationship will be the same and the questions asked may be similar, but the relationship of spiritual direction is not mutual. The director is there to listen to the directee. I first heard about the ministry of spiritual direction when I was in seminary. I recognized my need to have someone with whom to share my fears and doubts about where God was leading me. My director lived 45 minutes away from my home. I remember driving to see her one day, weeping with anticipation. Someone was waiting to listen to me with a compassionate heart, and nothing more than honesty would be asked of me. I needed that one-way relationship at that time.

You might wish to seek out a spiritual director, but in a praying congregation a spiritual friend may be available, for many folk will be attending to their prayer lives and their relationship to God. They will be as eager to share as you are. Let your heart lead you in your search for a spiritual friend. As you attend prayer classes and groups, pay attention to people who listen well, who respect different opinions, and who seem committed to their own life of prayer. You will want someone you trust and with whom you would be comfortable sharing your experiences. You will also want to select someone you would like to listen to, whose issues touch your soul. Imagine yourself talking with and listening to this person about emerging issues in your spiritual lives. Imagine how it would feel to share your deepest longings and to hear another's.

Asking someone to become your spiritual friend can feel risky. You may be afraid that the person will say no, or that they might say yes out of obligation. Remember that you are not only asking for friendship, you are offering friendship. The person you have selected may also be looking for a spiritual friend. When you approach someone with your invitation, be aware that she will need to go through her own discernment process. You may discover that the person you asked is as eager as you are for this spiritual friendship. However, you may have asked someone who is not willing to make a commitment at this time, or she might already have a soul friend. Although it is easy to take a refusal as a personal rejection, try not to fall into that trap. Both people in a spiritual friendship have to feel comfortable with each other and the commitment they are making.

A spiritual director or a soul friend may become important to you as you discover new longings to pray.

When two people explore becoming intentional soul friends, they need to decide what they want this relationship to look like. Like any relationship, it will evolve and deepen over time, but beginning guidelines are important. You will need to decide such questions as where, how often, and for how long you will meet. You will need to discuss your expectations of the role prayer will play in your friendship. Many spiritual friends begin their time together with spoken prayer offered by one or the other or both. Others begin their time with a period of silence. After some form of beginning prayer, soul friends might share with each other whatever spiritual issues are on their hearts. Their conversation may flow easily, so that both are speaking and listening as in any dialogue. Or they may take turns, with one person sharing for an allotted amount of time while the other listens, and then they switch. Most meetings of spiritual friends end with some kind of prayer and a commitment to pray for the other in the time apart.

Activity 5.4: Finding a Spiritual Friend

Time: Three sessions of 20 minutes each

Materials: Simple writing materials for participants. An excellent resource for this process is *Finding a Spiritual Friend: How Friends and Mentors Can Make Your Faith Grow* by Timothy Jones (Upper Room Books, 1998).

Looking for a spiritual friend is a process rather than an event. To help with the process, this activity is divided into three sessions. These shorter sessions can be combined with another activity if time allows. As the process continues, you may need to meet with some people individually to help them in their search for a spiritual friend or possibly a spiritual director.[3]

Discernment

- Discuss the difference between spiritual friendship and spiritual direction. Respond to any questions participants have.
- Invite everyone to reflect over the coming week on their desire to have a spiritual friend, their willingness to be a spiritual friend to another, or whether they feel this would be a good time to be with a spiritual director.

Sharing

- At the next session, invite sharing about their discernment. Remind them that the choice not to ask for or become a spiritual friend is a valid outcome of discernment.
- Discuss together how people are feeling about asking another to be a spiritual friend or the possibility that they may be invited into that relationship by someone else. Allow them to express any fears and doubts they may have.

- For those who have decided they want to find a spiritual director, give them guidance on how to do that.

Living Into the Relationship

- Give the group time to share about their experience of spiritual friendship or direction. They do not need to tell the name of their spiritual friend, but it would be helpful for others to know how the meetings have been structured and what the relationship means to their spiritual growth.
- Encourage them to think about ways to evaluate with their spiritual friend how the relationship is going. They might plan to ask each other periodically if both of them want the relationship to continue.
- Make yourself available to talk privately with anyone who needs guidance regarding their spiritual friendship.

Some congregations take names of those looking for spiritual friends and help church members find each other. This can be helpful in some cases but can be problematic if participants feel they are put with someone they do not want to be with and have no way to terminate the relationship. You would need to plan for the possibility of this happening.

Two pastors I know who live about an hour apart have become intentional spiritual friends. They meet once a month in a coffee shop halfway between their churches. When they get together, they catch up a little with the details of their lives. Then they pray together before one of them shares what is in his heart. His friend serves as

> *In a soul-friend relationship, the conversation does not need to be limited to prayer, for one's relationship with God extends into all areas of life.*

a listening presence, acknowledging feelings, asking clarifying questions, and simply opening his heart to the stories being told. He does not jump in with his own experiences, give advice, or try to solve his friend's problems. At the end, the listening friend may reflect back what he has heard the other say and may offer a suggestion of a new way to think about the issue. They close their time with silent prayer and arrange when to meet again. At the next meeting, they shift roles. The one who listened in the first meeting will then have the whole time to share while his friend listens deeply to him.

Spiritual friendship does not need to be as formally structured as these two pastors designed their meetings. Some people prefer to simply share with another informally. In a soul-friend relationship, the topic of conversation does not need to be limited to prayer, for one's relationship with God extends into all areas of life. The difference between a soul friend and other trusted friends is that in a spiritual friendship, when sharing issues of health, relationships, employment, or leisure, the presence of God is addressed. After a person has shared a concern about her daughter, a soul friend might ask her: "Have you prayed about this?" or "Do you trust God to love your daughter as she goes though this transition?" A spiritual friend is always willing to ask the questions or offer reflections honoring the other's relationship with God.

Being a spiritual friend is similar to becoming a teacher of prayer. Both roles hold at their core the willingness to listen to

God and others. Those who teach others to pray do not need to have perfected any particular prayer form, followed their rule of life faithfully, or mastered the spiritual classics. You may feel you are not qualified to teach others to pray and therefore be tempted to skip the next chapter. I urge you to read it, for I believe that anyone with a love for God and others can teach people to pray. You may discover that you too can become a teacher of prayer.

6

BECOMING A TEACHER OF PRAYER

Have you ever imagined that you would appear before a group to teach them about prayer? I know at one time I couldn't imagine it, and yet now I do it regularly. How did this happen? Not by any plan of mine! I wanted to teach others about spiritual direction because it was so powerful in my own life. I decided to explore the possibility of teaching at the Iliff School of Theology in Denver, where I had recently moved. I made an appointment to speak with the dean at Iliff about becoming adjunct faculty there. As we talked I suggested some ideas for a class in spiritual direction but quickly learned the seminary was not willing for someone unknown to them to design and present a new course. The dean did recognize the need to offer some spiritual formation classes, however, and made a proposal to me. "There's a course that hasn't been taught for a while. It's called 'The Life of Prayer.' Would you consider teaching that?"

My first thought was that I couldn't possibly teach that class. "Maybe a class called 'Explorations in Prayer,'" I countered. That title seemed safer. I could help students explore prayer, but to teach "The Life of Prayer" implied that I, the teacher, had a prayer life! Oh, I prayed, often haphazardly, but I wasn't sure it could be called a life of prayer. "No," the dean said. "We need to use the title and description we have. It's fairly general, though. You can just let it guide you—and then

96 A Praying Congregation

teach what you want. Let me know in the next few days." I realized our interview was over.

And so I began to teach about prayer. The more I taught, the more I learned. Students shared stories and experiences that enriched my understanding of prayer. They asked questions I couldn't answer, which made me search for new ideas. They invited me

By teaching from a place of vulnerability, I was learning about the goodness of God.

to teach in their churches, where I learned how members of their congregations were longing to pray. I met leaders who wanted their churches to become praying congregations. A mentor from my days in education once told me: "We teach best what we are trying to learn ourselves." This statement rang true as I began teaching prayer.

Even as I felt called to continue teaching and learning about prayer, I sometimes felt like a fraud. What was I doing teaching others to pray when I had no regular prayer practice? How could I teach about prayer when I had not formally studied the Christian mystics whose lives were filled with devotion and discipline and who were models of prayer? Did I have the wisdom to guide people into a deeper relationship with God when I was still confused about who God was?

I did not try to settle these doubts before I began to teach; rather, I wrestled with them as I taught. I knew if I waited to become an expert in prayer and get my own prayer life in order before I began teaching, I would never enter a classroom. So I forged ahead, including all my feelings, experiences, questions, and fears. Gradually I realized that by teaching from this inclusive place of vulnerability, I was learning what I needed to know—not only about prayer but about the goodness of God.

United Methodist bishop William Willimon wrote about biblical leadership: "God's choice [of teachers] tells us more about God than the positive qualities of the people who are called to [teach]."[1] God called the most unlikely people to serve. God did not call those with honed skills, fancy techniques, or a list of credentials. God chose Moses who could not speak clearly, Mary when she was young and innocent, and Peter who never seemed to understand what Jesus was talking about. What these inept leaders had in common was faith in God and the trust that they would be given the tools necessary to do what had been asked. God would give them the ability to lead and to teach. Their task was to serve gratefully with the gifts they had been given.[2]

Over many years of teaching and writing about prayer, I have become aware that God has given me what I have needed to do this ministry. I could not have done it on my own. God's gifts have come through my imagination, as in the times I have suddenly discovered a new image that helps me speak about prayer; they have come through other people with their questions, experiences, and invitations that stretch me into areas of discomfort; and they have come through the love of family, friends, and community who have encouraged and sustained me as my ministry unfolded. God has not granted me a perfect prayer life but an expanding one. There are times when I begin a presentation, wondering how I ever got to this place. That doubt reminds me to

> *Are you willing to consider that through God's grace, you are being invited to help your church become a praying congregation?*

breathe a prayer for guidance and to teach about the wonder and mystery of God as best I can.

Are you willing to imagine yourself teaching prayer, knowing that you do not understand everything, that your prayer life may be in disarray, that you have no formal training? Are you willing to consider that through God's grace, you are being invited to become a leader in helping your church become a praying congregation? To guide you in your discernment, the activities in the sidebars of this chapter are designed for your own reflection, rather than providing you with lessons for teaching others. Allow them to help you recognize your gifts for teaching and your willingness to become a teacher of prayer.

YOUR RELATIONSHIP WITH GOD

Central to the art of teaching prayer is the teacher's relationship with God. Author Marjorie Thompson writes: "Only from a relationship in which we know ourselves to be impossibly and improbably loved do we find the freedom to offer authentic spiritual leadership."[3] We may be quick to affirm God's love for others but wonder if we ourselves are loved. To know, truly know, that God loves us is a practice as well as a belief.

This practice includes becoming willing to receive the love that we believe God so freely offers. I often imagine God's love as a warm golden light surrounding others and the world, and large enough to encompass everything. But I know I often place myself outside that love, seeing it but not claiming it for myself. I need to remind myself that God's love is waiting for me. I have to choose to receive it. In my imagination I watch myself step forward into the light of love. I open all of who I am to this wondrous gift. For a moment I know that I am improbably and impossibly loved by God. And then I forget, the experience fades, and I find myself again outside the circle of God's love. I know I am outside when I do not respect myself, when I compare myself to others and find myself lacking, or when I disparage the gifts God has given me. Then I know it is time to practice choosing once again to step toward God's love. God offers; we must be actively willing to receive.

To know, truly know, that God loves us is a practice as well as a belief.

Through this or similar practices, you can strengthen your trust that God loves you. Grounded in God's love, you will be

ACTIVITY 6.1: THE COMPASSIONATE OBSERVER

Time: 30 minutes

Materials: Your journal or other writing material

Setting: A comfortable chair in a quiet place where you will be uninterrupted

This meditation is designed to help you compassionately examine the possibility of becoming a teacher of prayer. You might invite a spiritual friend to guide you through this activity. If you are doing it alone, you may wish to read through the instructions to see where you are headed before you begin the meditation. When you are comfortable, you can do the activity slowly and prayerfully.

Listing Your Gifts and Limitations

- On one sheet of paper or on a page in your journal, make a list of all the gifts and skills you have that help you know that you could become a teacher of prayer. You might include such qualities as your love of God, your ability to affirm other people's experiences, your experience teaching in other fields. Search deeply into your experience, naming as many qualities as you can. Be aware of how you feel as you make this list.
- On another sheet of paper, or on the opposite page of your journal, make a list of all the reasons you think you would be unable to be a teacher of prayer. You might include your fear of being wrong, your doubts about the way you pray, your lack of experience. Be aware of how you feel as you make this list.

Using Your Imagination

- Prepare yourself for a quiet reflection using the lists you have made. Attend to your breathing, calm your feelings, and quiet your mind.
- Imagine yourself teaching prayer with all the gifts and strengths you put on your first list. Imagine your facial expressions, body posture, and movements as you teach.

Become aware of how you feel as you teach and how your mind is working. Attend to ways the presence of God is made known through your teaching. Visualize yourself as clearly as possible. Be aware of how you feel as you watch yourself teach. Then let the image fade.

- Now imagine yourself teaching prayer from the place of your limitations. Pay attention to how your body looks now, the feelings you have, and the way your mind is working. Is the spirit of God present now in your teaching? If so, how is it made known? Be aware of how you feel as you watch yourself teach. Then let this image fade.

- Before the next step in the imagery process, take a deep breath and find a way to connect to your compassionate heart. You might remember a situation that evokes your compassion or imagine a flame deep within you. Allow the compassion to grow, and then open your heart so you can now see with the eyes of compassion. When you are ready, invite both teaching images to come into your mind's eye, seeing them side by side, and invite a dialogue between them. Allow your compassion to influence their interaction. Listen to what they have to say to each other. Watch as they find a way to teach together. When some resolution has emerged, let the image fade, and take all the time you need to write about your experience.

Questions for Reflection

- How did compassion help you see yourself more clearly?
- How could your gifts become liabilities? How could your limitations become gifts?
- How might both parts of yourself, working together, contribute to authentic teaching?

This meditation is not designed to give you answers, but rather to guide you to the position of the compassionate observer within. When you see yourself clearly and with compassion, you are more able to discern God's calling. You might practice this compassionate position as you read the rest of this chapter.[4]

able to learn to teach creatively with an open heart. You will not be as likely to become attached to your plans, rigid about your approach, or concerned about success. With deepening trust you can open yourself to the movement of the spirit, listen to participants' hearts, and share gently what knowledge and wisdom you have. Teaching *from* the love of God, rather than teaching *about* the love of God is particularly important when you are talking about prayer. The congruence of your words and actions encourages others to learn more about the possibilities of prayer and to risk drawing closer to God. As you teach more from this place, your own experiences of prayer may deepen.

EXPERIENCING PRAYER

The experience of your own prayer life needs to be the foundation from which you teach. This does not mean that the ways you pray must be settled, formal, or even consistent. Making your own prayer the foundation for teaching means that you are willing to continue to explore and deepen your relationship with God and to share your experiences with others. Teaching from your own prayer life means that you do not simply read and study a form of prayer before you teach it. You practice it long enough to be familiar with your experience of its blessings and difficulties.

A youth leader realized her haste to teach new ideas in her class of high school students when she was praying the intention described on page 79. She noticed how she would praise God with her hands raised, reach out for the blessings of the day, and then move directly to the motion that indicated sharing what she had received. She forgot to take the blessings into her heart before she began sharing. "That is a pattern of mine," she laughed. "I love new ideas, and when I find them I am so eager to teach them to the kids, I forget to practice them myself." The tendency to skip our own experience of prayer is a temptation for all those who teach others to pray.

You will not have stories to tell if you have not experienced the lessons you are teaching, whether you are introducing new prayer forms or inviting activities that prepare the heart for prayer. Have you recalled how you learned to pray? Have you examined your beliefs about prayer? What is your image of God, and how has it changed over time? Are you satisfied with your rule of life, or are you making adjustments? Your stories are not the heart of the teaching. God is always at the center. But the stories of your experiences enliven the lessons and let others see your foibles and your vulnerability, as well as your strength and wisdom. When you share honestly with a group, they know that continued exploration and practice of prayer is possible for them as well.

The experience of your own prayer life needs to be the foundation from which you teach.

I have found that groups love to hear the difficulties I have had with different forms of prayer, as well as those practices that have become part of my rule of life. When I teach centering prayer, I always let the group know that I rarely practice this form of prayer at home; however, I love to practice it in a group. I attend centering prayer retreats and welcome this form of prayer as I gather with colleagues for meetings. The intention of the group seems to keep me connected to my intention to simply be with God—something I am unable to do alone.

When I encourage a group to use crayons to draw images after they have participated in a guided visualization, I tell them the story of one of my seminary professors who required us to keep a journal every day for a month with no words, only images. That assignment released my fear of drawing and led me to understand the power of images in prayer. To this day, I include drawings and colors in many of my journal entries.

When introducing the practice of walking the labyrinth, students enjoy hearing how I got lost on a path that you are not supposed to get lost on. I had gone to Grace Cathedral in San Francisco to take a weekend workshop about the labyrinth with Lauren Artress, an Episcopal priest and psychotherapist whose work has brought this ancient practice to many people of faith. She gave us fascinating information about the origins and history of the labyrinth and was careful to explain that the labyrinth was not a maze. It was not designed to trick you. There was one path in and the same one out, and although there were twists and turns, and you often couldn't tell exactly where you were, if you kept walking you would arrive at the center. When you were ready, you would follow the same path out.

The cathedral was dark the night our group began our first walk. Music was playing and candles were burning. I entered the path and began to walk. I had no idea how long it would take to reach the center, but soon it seemed as if I had been walking a long time. I remembered Lauren's assurance that I could not get lost so I continued walking. I walked and walked and ended up at the entrance.

When we teach from our own experiences—drawing on our doubts as well as our faith—we engage the heart as well as the mind in the process.

I never did get to the center. How I got lost, I will never know, but I did take Lauren's admonition to heart—that everything that happens on the labyrinth is a metaphor for one's life.

When we teach from our own experiences—drawing on our difficulties and delights, our doubts as well as our faith—we engage the heart as well as the mind in the teaching and learning process. Our minds are important in teaching prayer, and the reading and studying we do is an integral part of the process. We do not want to teach without any intellectual understanding of our topic. If we try to teach others solely from what we have studied and read, however, we will bypass the wisdom of our bodies and feelings. Integrating our experiences of prayer into our lessons leads to authentic teaching that will touch the hearts of others.

TEACHING WITH INTEGRITY

Steve Doughty, author and pastor, writes that "to live with integrity is to be undivided. It is to stand complete and whole."[5] The same could be said for the art of teaching. To teach with integrity is to bring all of who we are to the task. We do not separate our inner and outer lives. We live publicly what we value privately. Our actions and our words are congruent. For example, I discovered what can go wrong when my words and actions aren't congruent. A friend of mine who was a Catholic priest asked me to teach a class for him in the local parish. I was just beginning to teach about prayer and was eager for the opportunity. "Do you think they will care that I'm not Catholic?" I asked him. "You don't need to tell them," he replied. I took his words as a command and decided to hide my Protestant affiliation.

That two-hour class was harder and seemed longer than any other teaching experience I had had before or have had since. I watched every word and monitored every response. I couldn't listen to the students, because I was so focused on myself. I didn't lie by telling them I was Catholic, but I lived a lie by denying my own heritage and pretending to be someone I wasn't. I knew at the end of class that I never wanted to teach that way again, for I knew I had not been authentic. My perception about how I had taught that day was affirmed the next week when my friend asked the class for a response to my teaching. One participant told him that she had enjoyed the material, but added that I was so formal and distant that she had a difficult time believing what I said.

Activity 6.2: Authentic Teaching

Time: 30 minutes

Materials: Your journal or other writing material

Setting: A comfortable place for reflection

This activity provides an opportunity to reflect on the experiences of prayer in your own life that would be foundational for your teaching. It then invites you to see if there are areas of prayer that you might welcome to broaden and strengthen your foundation of prayer.

Remembering

- In chapter 2 you were invited to remember how you learned to pray. Which of those early experiences do you think are part of your foundation of prayer?
- What other prayer experiences in your teenage or adult years are part of your own learning about prayer?
- How have you explored your relationship with God in ways that you may not have thought of as prayer but now realize were forms of prayer?
- Which of these memories might be appropriate to share in your teaching of prayer?

Stretching into New Experiences

- Are there prayer forms you have read about or studied but not practiced? Would you be willing to commit to praying that way for a period of time?
- Do you feel drawn to a form of prayer that you know little or nothing about? Would you be willing to pursue that new experience?

You may not be able to complete this activity in 30 minutes. Hold your reflections lightly over the next days and weeks, taking time to jot down your ideas. If you keep an open mind, you may discover hidden memories that take time to come forth. This ongoing reflection will serve your own deepening prayer life, as well as guide you to becoming an authentic teacher of prayer.[6]

That experience has taught me to pay close attention to what I include and what I leave out of my teaching. Participants in a class on prayer need to know the foundation of my teaching, so it is appropriate for me to tell them some of my early experiences of prayer and reveal the shape of my present

prayer life. If I share too little, they will not have a sense of who I am and where my ideas come from. However, I must not share indiscriminately. The group does not need all

Speaking my feelings aloud would be authentic, but would such a confession distract from my purpose?

the details of my life or what I am feeling every moment of my teaching. I need to weigh whether what I share is for the good of the lesson or whether it is satisfying some inner need of my own. Sometimes as I teach, I begin to worry about what is happening in the class, or I feel discouraged that it is not going the way I had planned, and I want to tell the class of my frustration. Speaking my feelings aloud would be authentic and honest, but I must ask myself whether the teaching of prayer will be enhanced by my revelation, or if such a confession will distract from my purpose. Might the class begin to worry about my feelings and my process, rather than attending to their own experience of prayer? By sharing too much, we risk making our ministry more about us than about God.

I witnessed a preacher make this mistake when he turned the attention of the congregation to his own process and away from what God may have been revealing through his sermon. I remember listening to him preach, not always following him but being touched by some of his stories and insights. He gave me a lot to think about. After the sermon he came down from the pulpit and stood in front of the congregation and said: "I'm really sorry. That sermon just didn't work. I was trying something new, but I couldn't carry it off. I hope you'll forgive me." I was stunned. My first thought was how honest he was being. Then I was angry. His sermon had revealed a little more about God to me, and he was taking my sacred experience and making it about him. He was ignoring the possibility that God could be heard through an imperfect instrument. He was telling us that because he believed he had failed, God's love and wisdom could not be heard. His behavior revealed that he was living as a "functional atheist."

Parker Palmer, Quaker author and teacher, wrote that functional atheism is "the belief that ultimate responsibility for everything rests with us."[7] We may believe in God, talk about God, worship God, pray to God, and then we act as if God does not exist. Functional atheism is a risk for all teachers but particularly dangerous for teachers of prayer. How authentic are we if we talk about the wonder of God's love, encourage others to open their hearts to the possibility of a deeper relationship with God, and help them explore their interdependence with God and then teach as if their learning were completely up to us? We must remember that our task is to teach as authentically and effectively as possible, and then let go and trust that the spirit of God will do the rest.

> *We may believe in God, worship God, pray to God— and then we act as if God does not exist.*

I am often humbled when I realize how God acts through what I experience as my teaching mistakes. One time a student asked me a question during the class time that was not relevant to the topic at hand. I asked him if we could come back to the issue later. He was agreeable, but I forgot, and never responded to his concern. The next week he told me that another student in the class had come to him, saying that she shared his question and concern and asked if they could they spend some time talking together. He was excited by the exchange and said that their dialogue was for him the most valuable part of the class.

An important part of teaching with integrity is listening to your congregation. You may be eager to lead, but they may not be ready to follow. You may be excited about teaching a six- to ten-week class entitled "Becoming a Praying Congregation" using the ideas, stories, and lessons in this book. Or you might want to cover the material by inviting members of a study group to read the chapters and take turns leading the lessons. However, neither of these approaches may be the best for your church. The members may not be ready for an in-depth study, they may have expressed a desire for information on a particular method of prayer, or perhaps they have been asking for a retreat. You may have realized through experience that many in your congregation have been resistant to integrating prayer into the life of the church. In any of these cases, you would be wise to find another way to involve your church in the exploration of prayer.

Teaching with integrity calls us to a radical trust in God. We study the material, prepare our lessons, call on our experience to enliven our teaching, and then we let go. We are not attached to our own success or with making sure the students learn what we think they should. Surrendering to God, we allow the spirit to be alive in the classroom. When we teach with integrity, we know that no matter how knowledgeable, experienced, and prepared we are, the students' learning is not ultimately in our hands. Such is the wonder and the mystery of God!

EMBRACING MYSTERY

No matter how much we know about God, our relationship to God, and the ways we deepen and strengthen that relationship, prayer remains a mystery. Teaching people to pray calls us to share all we know even while we embrace our not knowing. This balance is difficult to maintain and if we are not careful we

Activity 6.3: Alternative Lessons

Time: As long as it takes

The following suggestions are ways you might weave some of the lessons of this book into a prayer program designed for your unique congregation.

1. Introduce activity 2.1: "Memories of Learning to Pray" in a variety of settings. It could be done fairly quickly at the beginning of a meeting or an existing class. This will begin to get people talking.

2. Offer a three-hour class on one of the methods of prayer in chapter 7. But before you present the information and provide time to practice the prayer, invite the participants to remember how they learned to pray and then engage them in activity 3.1: "Beliefs About Prayer."

3. In a class that is in process, share activity 1.1: "Creating Safety," then teach the members of the group a method of dialogue using activity 1.2: "The Talking Stick."

4. Offer a two- or three-week class entitled "Healing Your Image of God," using activity 4.1 as a starting point.

5. Encourage members of your congregation to practice praying out loud by teaching the method described in chapter 7 on page 132. Practice time could come at the beginning of a class on a topic other than prayer.

6. Offer a class on "A Rule of Life," inviting the participants into activity 5.1: "Renewing Your Spirit," and then guiding them to create their own rule of life.

7. In a church publication, describe the role of spiritual friends and spiritual directors and the important part they can play in spiritual formation. Invite anyone interested in becoming part of such a relationship to meet with you individually. Help those who come discern their need and guide them to finding the right person.

8. Introduce embodied prayer into your worship services by teaching the congregation the movements to the Lord's Prayer found on page 119. If your congregation is not ready for this activity, invite a small group to express the prayer through movement while the rest of those in worship say the words out loud.

To discover ways to encourage prayer in your congregation, listen to the needs of the people. Honor where they are and what their next step might be. Move forward slowly and gently, yet be willing to challenge them to stretch into new experiences. Be creative, and let the spirit guide you. Watch for those in the congregation who are already teaching prayer through their example, their stories, and the questions they ask. Help them to recognize their gifts, and invite them to join you in leadership. Everyone in a praying congregation can become a teacher of prayer.

can slip to one side or the other. I have heard some teachers try to explain in detail exactly how they believe prayer works. I have heard others abdicate responsibility by throwing up their hands and saying, "Why talk about it? It's all a mystery!"

One way to stay in balance is to be willing to teach from our experience and at the same time be willing to say, "I don't know!", "I'm not sure," or "I don't understand." I can speak with confidence about God's love for us and about God's spirit empowering us to create peace and justice in the world, because I have experienced that love and empowerment. But if someone asks me to prove it or define it, I am willing to admit that I can't. "I just *know*," I say. "I can't explain it; I just know."

I learned how to stay with my experience and not try to convince another of the wonder and the power of prayer from my younger stepson. He asked me one day why I believed in God. Because of his antireligious stance at that time, I could tell he was preparing his arguments to counter anything I had to say. So I took a deep breath and answered with a truth I did not know I knew: "I believe in God, because I would rather live my life in relationship with a merciful God than without such a connection. I choose to believe in God." He could not argue with my choice. I had nothing to prove, only something wonderful to share. And that is finally what teaching prayer is all about—simply sharing the wonder of God.

7

TEACHING PRAYER FORMS AND SPIRITUAL PRACTICES

A praying congregation responds to people's longing to pray and their experiences and questions about prayer. The church prepares members' hearts so they are able to receive new information about specific prayer forms and spiritual practices and discover ways to integrate this knowledge into their daily lives. As individuals and groups seek to deepen their relationship with God they may request guidance about a particular method of prayer. Maybe they have heard about centering prayer and want to know what it is and how to do it. Others might be interested in more informal ways to pray and ask for instruction. Members of a prayer chain or some other structure for prayers of intercession may desire ongoing instruction and encouragement. One large church offers this instruction in the form of a retreat held once a year. The retreat is an opportunity to invite new people to join the ministry and also to delve more deeply into the experiences and questions surrounding intercessory prayer.

Congregational leaders, both clergy and lay, may want to provide their parishioners with an opportunity to explore a prayer form or spiritual practice that is completely new to them. A lay leader in a rural church went to a retreat where he learned about *Lectio Divina,* the ancient practice of praying with Scripture. Wanting to share his delight in this new practice, he offered a four-week class during the adult Sunday school hour. Many people were eager to learn this new form of prayer. They were amazed at how profound praying with the Bible could be.

In teaching prayer and spiritual practices to groups over many years, I have discovered three important principles for the process. The first is to begin the teaching with a brief introduction to the prayer form. Participants do not need a history of the origins of the prayer form, detailed lessons about what others have written about it, or even much about the leader's own experience with the prayer form. This information can come later if the group requests it. In the beginning, they simply need enough information to participate in the prayer itself.

A praying congregation responds to people's longing to pray.

The method of prayer you are teaching may be familiar to some and completely new to others. In my experience, this difference in knowledge and experience does not cause problems. In fact, I have found the variety to be a benefit. After I give my introduction and before we begin praying together, I invite those who are familiar with the prayer form to add anything to my instructions that they think others might find helpful. This invitation acknowledges that others in the group have knowledge and wisdom to share about the prayer form we are learning. Those for whom the practice is new receive insights from different perspectives and learn that there is never one right way to pray.

The second principle is to offer the group the opportunity to practice the prayer form together. This time of prayer is at the heart of teaching prayer and building a praying congregation. I have discovered that many people may want to hear, read, and talk about prayer—without ever taking time to pray.

If they go home without experiencing the practice of prayer together, they are not likely to practice alone. The group prayer time is the foundation for continued prayer. Individuals leave class with the knowledge that they have taken the first step in practicing a new prayer form or deepening a practice they had previously begun.

Providing a time for sharing after the common prayer experience is the third principle. I ask the participants to share their experience of the prayer. They can talk about how they felt during the prayer, questions that came to mind and heart, and how they might practice this prayer form in their lives. The sharing can be done in small groups of three or four or with the group as a whole. In either case, I encourage dialogue so that others besides me can offer answers and thoughts. I often end the session with a suggestion of how they might practice during the weeks to come.

For each of the methods of prayer described in this chapter, I will share with you the information, stories, and images that I use in my introductory teaching. This will be followed by an invitation to pray, so that you will have a way to begin guiding your group into a common prayer experience. If you have your own ideas about how to practice the prayer, please use those. What is important is that the group prays together, even if only for a very brief time. In the dialogue following the practice, allow the group's experiences and questions to guide you. You might be prepared to offer some more information if the group requests it. For further study, I have provided the titles and authors of some books that have been helpful to me and that I often recommend to members of a group if they ask.

> *Group prayer by the class is the foundation for continued prayer by individuals.*

You may be reading this book to learn more about your own prayer life and do not anticipate teaching others to pray. If that is true for you, use the following information as an individual lesson written just for you. Read the introductory information about the prayer, then practice the prayer form alone. You might journal about your experience, writing down your impressions and feelings as well as questions that arise. If you want more information about the prayer, you could read about it in the books recommended or others you may know of. Be careful about the tendency many of us have to read about prayer rather than praying. Books and classes are helpful, but the only way to truly learn to pray is to pray.

INTERCESSORY PRAYER

Prayers of intercession ask God to intercede in our lives, our communities, and the life of the world. Intercessory prayer is one of the most common forms of prayer. It is included in almost all liturgies in the Christian tradition. As we discussed in chapter 4, our theology will determine our understanding of how God responds to these prayers, but whatever our image of God, we are often moved to offer intercessory prayers.

An image that has been helpful for me in trying to understand prayers of intercession comes from Douglas Steere, a Quaker philosopher. Steere likened the process of intercessory prayer to the lowering of a threshold. He wrote that when intercessory prayers are offered, the threshold in the other person is lowered "to make the besieging love of God . . . slightly more visible and more inviting."[1] The threshold that Steere refers to is our resistance, often unconscious, to experiencing God's loving presence. Steere also wrote that when we pray for others and the world, our own thresholds are lowered and we become more available to God's besieging love. Therefore, intercessory prayer affects the hearts and lives of others while transforming our own hearts. The prayer does not bring God to the person or the situation, for God is already there. The prayer does not convince or manipulate God, for God's intention for whole-ness and healing, peace and justice, is unwavering.

When we hold this image we do not have to figure out how to pray for another. Often we do not pray because we do not know what to pray for. Does the ill person need patience? A miracle cure? Does the marriage need saving? Or a peaceful divorce? Do the victims of an earthquake need courage? Or maybe help and compassion from neighboring countries? In our confusion, we often do not pray. But if we use the image of the threshold, it does not matter how or for what we pray. We can simply pray whatever is in our hearts without worry of whether it is right or wrong. Our heartfelt prayers will serve to lower the defenses in those prayed for, and God's besieging love will become more visible and inviting.

Prayer Practice

Most liturgical prayers of intercession are verbal. This practice of prayer uses the imagination and is done silently. You may wish to light a candle to separate the teaching of prayer from the practice of prayer. Invite the group to enter into an attitude of prayer. When you feel they are ready, ask them to imagine a person they wish to pray for. As they visualize, encourage them to see that person surrounded by the light of God's besieging love. Have them hold that image for a few moments and then allow another person to come to mind, again surrounded by the light of God's love. Invite them to continue with this imagery at their own speed, spending as long as they wish with one person or another, or moving more quickly through the many people in their lives they wish to pray for. You might end this practice of intercessory prayer with quietly spo-ken words, such as: "For these people for whom we have prayed, and for all others who need our prayers, we ask your blessing, gracious God. Amen."

Further Resources

Jane E. Vennard, *Praying for Friends and Enemies*, Minneapolis: Augsburg Books, 1995.
Walter Wink, *The Powers That Be: Theology for a New Millennium*, Minneapolis: Augsburg Fortress, 1998.

BODY PRAYER

The idea of praying with our bodies often makes people nervous. They are afraid they are going to be asked to use their bodies in ways that might embarrass them. Those who are physically challenged may be particularly anxious. Therefore, I always begin teaching about this form of prayer by naming those concerns and fears and reassuring the group that most everyone feels this way and that they will not have to engage in anything that makes them uncomfortable. Then I remind them of all the ways they already pray with their bodies. They may stand for hymns or the reading of the Gospel. Some kneel for prayer. They often come forward and reach out their hands to receive communion. They may use their voices to sing and their hands to pass the peace or place their offering in the collection basket. We are already embodied pray-ers.

In addition to using our bodies to express our prayers, we can learn to use our senses to become more attentive to God. If we open our senses, we may be surprised how often we are reminded of the presence of God in our lives. The taste of hot tea, the comforting touch of a friend, the smell of spring flowers, the sight of a loved one, the sound of early morning birds—all can serve to let us know that God is with us. Our breath can serve to remind us of the closeness of God's spirit. Our heartbeat can assure us of God's constant love.

Prayer Practice

For a common experience of a body prayer, you might lead the group in the morning prayer of intention that I described on page 79. Or you could teach them the following movements to accompany the Lord's Prayer:

> Our Father *(Hands out in front, palms up, waist high.)*
>
> Who art in heaven *(Hands raised as if to heaven.)*
>
> Hallowed be thy name *(Hands pressed together in traditional prayer position.)*
>
> Thy kingdom come *(Right hand reaches out to the side and scoops inward.)*
>
> Thy will be done *(Left hand reaches out to the side and scoops inward.)*
>
> On earth *(Palms down, waist high, moving as if playing in the dirt.)*
>
> As it is in heaven *(Palms upward at waist height, because heaven is here as well as above.)*
>
> Give us this day our daily bread *(Hands stretched out in front, cupped to receive.)*
>
> And forgive us our trespasses *(Right hand out straight to the side at shoulder level.)*
>
> As we forgive those who trespass against us *(Same movement with left hand.)*
>
> Lead us not into temptation *(Hands above head with wrists crossed as if bound.)*
>
> But deliver us from evil *(Break hands open as if being freed from bondage.)*
>
> For thine is the kingdom *(Hands upturned at waist.)*
>
> The power *(Hands at shoulder level, palms facing out with fingers spread.)*
>
> And the glory forever *(Hands raised and shaking, trembling as if making shooting stars.)*
>
> Amen *(Hands pressed together in traditional prayer position, head bowed.)*[2]

After the group has learned the movements, invite them to pray this prayer first with everyone speaking the words together, and then silently without words, letting the body pray by itself.

Further Resources

Flora S. Wuellner, *Prayer and the Body,* Nashville: Upper Room Books, 1987.

Jane E. Vennard, *Praying with Body and Soul,* Minneapolis: Augsburg Books, 2000.

ARROW PRAYERS

Arrow prayers are informal prayers spoken aloud or silently in our hearts in the midst of our daily life. They are so named because it has been said that these fervent prayers fly straight to the heart of God. The most common arrow prayers are "Help!" and "Thank you!" Sometimes we are struck suddenly by something awesome or horrible, and we utter, "Oh, my God!" When a family member or friend slips into our mind during the day we might breathe, "Be with him." "Enfold her." If a worry begins to distract us from other endeavors, we could ask God: "Relieve me." When we feel lonely or afraid, we might ask for companionship: "Jesus, walk with me."

Many people discount arrow prayers, believing they are not "real" prayers because they are uttered in desperation or in great joy and almost without thinking. I understand them to be a sign that we trust God's presence in our lives and the life of the world. I wonder whether these spontaneous prayers are pulled from us by God. Arrow prayers are ways we can stay aware of our relationship with God in the midst of daily activities.

Prayer Practice

In preparation for a time of prayer together, ask participants to remember arrow prayers they often use. They might also think of arrow prayers that they think could be useful to them. Invite them to share their arrow prayers with one another, during which time someone might hear just the prayer they need but were unable to think of by themselves. When everyone has two or three arrow prayers in mind, invite the group to pray them out loud together at the same time. Invite them to pray the same prayers over and over, varying the volume, the tone, and the speed of the words. There will be a cacophony of sound in the room, and at times individuals will want to simply listen. Encourage the prayers to continue until the voices begin to slow and quiet. When the group is still, let the silence linger, then close the prayer with a brief prayer such as, "We offer these prayers from our heart to yours, merciful God. Help us to pray them all through our days. Amen."

Musical Prayer

"The person who sings prays twice" is an old saying that links music to prayer. This connection is recognized by those people who place making music or listening to music on the list of things they do to nurture their spirit. They may be referring to singing hymns or listening to sacred music, but many find spiritual nurture in other forms of music as well. Picking out a new song on his guitar is a favorite prayerful activity for one man. Drumming in community brings a young woman closer to God. Writing and performing Christian rap helps two young men worship God. Attending the symphony touches a retired teacher's soul.

Having no musical training and not being able to carry a tune, I thought this form of prayer was not for me. I felt awkward singing even the most familiar hymns; my mind wandered when I listened to any style of music; I was embarrassed by not being able to tell what instruments were making which sounds. And then years ago on retreat I was introduced to chanting.

The chants we were taught came from the Taizé community in southern France. This unique ecumenical monastic community was founded in 1940 to establish a bridge between French and German Christians. The community later expanded to include efforts for reconciliation between Catholics and Protestants. The Taizé brothers are committed to working with the poor, and they welcome visitors from all over the world to join with them in their ministry and to study Scripture and worship God together. Chanting is an integral part of their daily worship. The chants are simple phrases frequently repeated, usually in Latin, although modern languages are sometimes used. Most importantly, the chants are easily sung.[3]

Prayer Practice

There may be someone in your congregation who knows the chants of Taizé and can lead a group in singing. However, live music is not necessary to discover the joy of chanting our prayers. Many CDs are available that are easily followed by a group. When you have chosen two or three chants, invite the group into a time of musical prayer. You might light a candle at the center of a circle or in the front of the room, if the chairs are in rows. Ask the group to prepare their hearts for prayer, and offer a few words of intention such as, "Holy God, may our prayers rise like incense before you" (based on Ps. 141:2). After the first chant, provide at least three minutes of silence before beginning the next one. Offer more silence at the end before a brief closing prayer.

Further Resources

David Steindl-Rast and Sharon Lebell, *The Music of Silence: Entering the Sacred Space of Monastic Experience*, San Francisco: Harper Publishing, 2001. This book comes with a chant CD.

W. A. Mathieu, *The Listening Book: Discovering Your Own Music,*
   Boston: Shambala Press, 1991.

Laudate: Music of Taizé, Veritas Productions, 1984. Compact
   disc that is easy to sing and contains a number of chants in
   English.

CENTERING PRAYER

Centering prayer is an ancient form of Christian prayer that has
been made available to contemporary Christians by the work
of Father Thomas Keating, a Cistercian monk. This method of
prayer helps us to simply rest in the presence of God. We do
not offer praise; we do not make requests. We simply rest in
God. Father Keating calls centering prayer "hanging out with
God."

To practice this prayer, you first need to select a sacred
word, sometimes called a prayer word. The word is to remind
you of your intention to be with God during your silent time.
Choose something that guides you into God's presence such
as *spirit, trinity, holy one, rest, return,* or *God.* Some people prefer to select an image, such as a well, a rainbow, a tree, or the
face of Jesus. When you have decided on your word, plan a
time when you can be uninterrupted for 20 minutes. Sit in a
comfortable chair where you are upright and supported. Begin
your prayer time with a brief word of scripture such as, "Be
still, and know that I am God!" (Ps. 46:10) or "My soul thirsts
for God" (Ps. 42:2).

And then simply sit, holding lightly your intention to be
present to God. Very soon, in probably less than a minute if
you are like me, your mind will begin to wander. You may
think of what you will have for lunch or when to pick up your
children. You may have a creative idea for a sermon, a lesson,
or a poem. You may begin to feel anxious, uncomfortable, or
bored and wonder what in the world you are doing sitting there

when you have so much else to do. Simply notice whatever thought or feeling takes you away from your intention to be with God, then silently say your sacred word and return to your intention.

The sacred word is not a mantra. A mantra is a word or phrase repeated over and over to quiet your thoughts and relax your mind. In centering prayer the sacred word is only used when you realize that you have moved away from your desire to be with God. The word is used to bring you back to your original intention. If your mind wanders so often that you have to say your sacred word hundreds of times, you may feel as if you are saying a mantra. In centering prayer, however, the intent of the sacred word is completely different. It does not serve to push away thoughts, but serves to bring us closer to God.

> Like other forms of prayer, centering prayer draws us more fully into the world.

Emptying the mind of thoughts is not the purpose of centering prayer. During your prayer time, your thoughts will continue to come and go. Your task is not to get caught by them. You let them go by like clouds in the sky, noticing they are there, but staying beneath them, not engaged in them, while you rest in the presence of God. When you do get hooked by your thoughts, you recognize what has happened and gently return to your original intention by invoking your sacred word.

Centering prayer is simple but not easy. It is foreign to those of us who have been brought up to be active and productive. It calls us to a practice that is often counter to much of what we have been taught about prayer. We can get discouraged after periods of centering when we feel that nothing has happened or when the prayer time was unpleasant and made us anxious. But Father Keating would tell us to persevere. He would say that what happens or does not happen in those 20 minutes is not the issue. Centering prayer is about spending time with God and opening ourselves to the transforming power of God's grace. Results may not be seen in the prayer period, but over time the fruit of prayer will be realized in our daily lives. We may become more attentive to God in every moment, realize that we have let go of an old resentment, or discover a depth of compassion we had never known before. Like other forms of prayer, centering prayer draws us more fully into the world.

Prayer Practice

Invite the group into a period of centering prayer together. If 20 minutes seems too long for a group just beginning, you might shorten it to 10 or 15 minutes. Begin the prayer time with a brief passage of scripture, and end it with a chime rung three times or with the words of the Lord's Prayer. Give the group some silent time before they engage in conversation.

Further Resources

Contemplative Outreach is an organization dedicated to the teaching and practice of centering prayer. There are chapters throughout the United States and in some other countries. You can access their information at: www.contemplativeoutreach.org.

Thomas Keating, *Open Mind, Open Heart: The Contemplative Dimension of the Gospel,* New York: The Continuum Publishing Company, 1998.

LECTIO DIVINA

Lectio Divina is a Latin phrase that means sacred reading. It is a method used to pray with the Bible. Often we read the Bible to learn about the history of the Hebrew people and the early Christians. We read the stories and the sayings of Jesus, trying to understand who he was and what relevance he has for us today. Praying with the Bible takes us away from this common form of reading for information. We slow our reading, savoring the words, allowing them to contribute to our spiritual formation.

When praying with the Bible, choose a short passage and read it multiple times. The first time you read the passage, listen to it as if you were hearing it anew, letting the words touch you in whatever way they will. This reading is called *lectio*. The second time you read the passage, think about all you know about this passage. You might examine the passages that come before and after it and think about when it may have been written and who the intended audience was. You may look at the literary style to see if it is history, a story, a prayer, or a letter. If you have access to different Bibles, you could explore the various translations. This reading is called *meditatio*. The third reading, *oratio*, allows the word to touch the heart, and you are invited to respond in prayer. You might speak, write, sing, draw, or dance your prayer. Express to God what the passage has evoked in your heart.

> *By praying with the Bible, we slow our reading, savoring the words, allowing them to contribute to our spiritual formation.*

The fourth reading, called *contemplatio*, invites you to rest in the passage and to allow the passage to rest in you. Simply sit, as in centering prayer, in the presence of God as revealed through Scripture. A Baptist preacher summarized from his own experience the first four steps of *lectio divina* by saying: "I read myself full, I think myself clear, I pray myself hot, and I let myself go!" Some teachers add a fifth reading that they call *incarnatio*. This reading allows you to reflect on living out the Bible passage or learnings you have received from Scripture in your daily life.

Reading and responding in these five ways, in a linear fashion, uses the scholastic form of *lectio divina*. If you skip around among the five ways of readings, maybe even reading the same way twice, you are using the monastic method of *lectio divina*. When teaching this form of prayer, I find it best to begin with the scholastic method. The clear structure helps students recognize and experience the specific intention of the different readings. I have also noticed the tendency in myself and others, whether praying the scholastic or the monastic style, to skip *contemplatio*. Be intentional about the resting, not only during the prayer time, but also during the days that follow. As the passage rests in your heart, you continue to be formed by the healing grace of God.

A slightly different form of *lectio divina* is attributed to Martin Luther. When asked by a friend how to pray with the Bible, he gave the following advice. Pick a short passage from Scripture and read it through once, listening for an overall sense of meaning. The second time you read it, ask yourself what it has to teach you. After the third reading, give thanks for the instruction you have received. Allow the fourth reading to guide you to confession. The fifth reading leads you to reflect on the guidance you have received from the passage and to rest in the assurance that even if you do not understand it completely, the way will be made clear.[4] This method of *lectio divina* provides more structured guidelines for the prayers and may be a good place to begin your teaching.

Prayer Practice

Choose one of the methods of *lectio divina* and a brief scripture passage to pray together with your group. It is helpful if every participant has a Bible, and a variety of translations makes the prayer more interesting. Read the passage aloud for the first time, reminding the group what to listen for. Invite someone with a different translation to read the same passage aloud a second time. As the group thinks about the passage in the scholastic method, or listens for instruction in Martin Luther's design, invite brief sharing within the group. Then ask a different person for each subsequent reading, reminding the group what they are listening for in each phase. Invite silence before each reader begins. In the reading that invites rest, allow the words to lead into silence with no dialogue or sharing. Let the group know how long the silence will be. When it is over, signal the end of *contemplatio* with a chime or a bell.

Further Resources

Thelma Hall, RC, *Too Deep for Words: Rediscovering Lectio Divina,* New York: Paulist Press, 1988.

Martin Smith, *The Word Is Very Near You: A Guide to Praying with Scripture,* Cambridge, Mass.: Cowley Publications, 1989.

M. Robert Mulholland Jr., *Shaped by the Word: The Power of Scripture in Spiritual Formation,* Nashville: Upper Room Books, 2000.

GRATITUDE

Theologian Karl Barth wrote that "gratitude is the precise creaturely counterpart to the grace of God."[5] David Steindl-Rast, a Benedictine monk, wrote: "To bless whatever there is, and for no other reason but simply because it is, that is what we are made for as human beings."[6] Both of these writers indicate that an integral part of our humanness is to give thanks to God. They call us to prayers of thanksgiving and the ongoing practice of gratitude. Even in the most difficult and trying circumstances, we can find something to be grateful for. When times are hard and we struggle with pain and loss, we are not grateful for the suffering, but we can open our eyes and hearts to our total reality and find one tiny spot of light in the midst of the darkness. When we do, we give thanks.

If gratitude is not your natural stance in life, you might begin this practice by keeping a gratitude journal. Most every night, take a few minutes to look back over your day to see the things for which you are grateful. They may be as small as a glimpse of a smiling baby or the feel of sunshine on your back. They may be as large and important as reconciling with an estranged friend, receiving a new opportunity, or witnessing the returning health of a loved one. Write them all, and over time your heart will grow in its capacity to see and record joy. You may be surprised how this attitude of gratitude can influence your experience and response to the world. You may find yourself offering prayers of gratitude during the day.

Prayer Practice

Invite your group into a prayer circle of gratitude. Prayers can begin with "I give thanks," "I am grateful for," or "I thank God for." Tell the participants to use whatever language is comfortable for them and to fill up the circle with their gratitude. When it seems that all has been said, encourage them to look deeper and further to find more and more that they are grateful for. Remind them to allow the prayers of others to trigger their own prayers of thanksgiving. This prayer circle may become joyous and rowdy at times, quiet and serious at others. Let the rhythm guide the group, and end with a brief closing prayer of gratitude that embraces all that has been said.

Further Resources

David Steindl-Rast, *Gratefulness: The Heart of Prayer*, New York: Paulist Press, 1984.

WORK AND SERVICE

Prayer deepens and strengthens our relationship with God. This holy connection is not only for the glory of God and our own spiritual development. Our relationship with God calls us into the world to work and to serve. We are God's hands, feet, and voices in the world. We are God's partner in creating the reign of God.

Connecting prayer with work and service does not necessarily mean praying while we work, although we might. Grounded in our relationship with God and holding the intention to include God in all we do, the work itself becomes prayer. Father Joe, the focus of author Tony Hendra's memoir, likens prayer to "work done as well as possible. Work done for others first and yourself second. Work you are thankful for. Work you enjoy. . . . Work that celebrates existence, whether it's growing grain in the fields or using God-given skills. . . . All this is prayer that binds us together and therefore to God."[7]

We are God's hands, feet, and voices in the world. We are God's partner in creating the reign of God.

The topics of work and service often feel like huge issues. The work we do to support ourselves and our loved ones does take a large portion of our time and energy. But that is not the only work and service to which we are called. We are called to partnership with God in other ways as well. These activities may involve charity work, political activism, advocating for justice, or caring for those in our community who are grieving or ill. In addition, we may offer small acts of service that are often unseen and rarely acknowledged, what Quaker author Richard Foster names "hidden services."[8]

One hidden service is common courtesy. Treating others politely may seem inconsequential, but remember how good you feel when you are treated with courtesy on the road, in stores, on the street, and in your home. Another is the service of listening, taking time to become for another a listening heart. Deep listening is more healing than answers quickly given to the concerns or questions of another. Hospitality is also a form of service that is hidden when there is no bold invitation but rather an offer of hospitality of the heart. Do we greet the strangers in our midst with open hearts? Do we see them with the eyes of Christ? And finally, we may offer service by allowing ourselves to be served. When we receive service from another we give an invisible gift. We make it possible for the other to serve.

Prayer Practice

Gather the group into a prayer circle and invite them into an attitude of prayer. Ask them to think of the different types of work they do in the world and to reflect on ways they might make this work more prayerful. How might God help them transform their work to prayer? Invite prayers for help to be spoken aloud. After a period of silence, ask the group to reflect on the hidden ways they serve in the world and in which areas they need God's help. Invite them to speak these prayers aloud. After another period of silence, invite the group to stand. Explain that you will begin a prayer of blessing that will continue around the circle. Turn to the person on your left and raise your hands, placing them on his shoulders. Offer the following blessing or something similar: "We bless the work and service you do in the world to build up the kingdom of God." That person receives the blessing and then turns to the next and repeats the blessing, continuing around the circle until you receive the final blessing. You might end the prayer time by holding hands and reciting the Lord's Prayer.

Further Resources

Richard Foster, "The Discipline of Service." Chapter 9 in *Celebration of Discipline: The Path to Spiritual Growth,* San Francisco: HarperSanFrancisco, 1998.

Jeffrey K. Salkin, *Being God's Partner: How to Find the Hidden Link Between Spirituality and Your Work,* Woodstock, Vt.: Jewish Lights Publishing, 1994.

Jane E. Vennard, *Embracing the World: Praying for Justice and Peace*, San Francisco: Jossey-Bass, 2003.

Praying Out Loud

A high percentage of North Americans list public speaking as one of the things they are most afraid of. I believe most people are also afraid of praying out loud. Although some churches encourage and expect all their members to be able to offer a prayer at any time for any situation, most of us do not have that experience in our background. Part of becoming a praying congregation is helping members become willing and able to spontaneously pray out loud. To do this they need to practice offering prayers in public in a safe and intimate setting.

Prayer Practice

Divide those willing to learn to pray out loud into groups of three or four. Give them an opportunity to speak to each other about their fears and ask any questions they may have about leading others in prayer. The sharing helps them realize that they are all nervous about the activity and builds support and compassion for one another. Ask one person in each group to indicate her willingness to pray out loud. When all the groups are ready, give the pray-ers a situation that calls for prayer. Begin with a fairly simple request. You might say: "You are at a neighbor's home for dinner, and you are asked to bless the food." Or, "At a church meeting you are asked to open the group with a prayer." The person prays out loud with her small group.

After the prayer has been offered in each group, allow the one who prayed to share her experience of praying out loud. Then invite the others in the group to speak of their experience. What did they like about it? Do they have any encouragement to offer? This discussion is to focus on the positive, building up the pray-er's confidence. If it seems appropriate, some gentle suggestions might be made. After the sharing in the small groups is completed, respond to questions or comments in the large group. When the general discussion in finished, have each group select a new pray-er. Invite them back into an attitude of prayer, and give the new person the opportunity to pray out loud with a different prayer request.

Offering people a variety of situations where prayers may be requested keeps this activity interesting and creative. These are some that I have used: "You visit a friend who is sick, and she asks you to pray with her." "At the hospital, a family member of someone facing serious surgery asks you to pray for the operation to be successful." "A mother whose son is in trouble asks you to pray for him." "During a baby shower, the expectant mother asks you to lead the group in prayer for the health and safe delivery of the child." When you have run out of ideas, let the group propose situations that they can think of in which they might be invited to pray.

A praying congregation helps members become willing and able to spontaneously pray out loud.

This activity is best done over a period of time. In an ongoing class or in a group that meets regularly, practicing praying out loud can become an integral part of the time spent together. No one is ever forced to take a turn, but even the most hesitant people usually volunteer when they realize how safe and affirming the small group is and as they see others grow from the experience. "I didn't think I would ever be able to pray out loud," is what one man said after he took his turn, "but I tried it, and my group told me how appropriate and heartfelt my prayer was." As practice continues and people become more confident, they may be willing to pray in front of larger groups. Take every opportunity to invite others to pray out loud in a variety of settings.

GOING DEEPER

As you have read these introductions to different forms of prayer with the accompanying prayer practices, I imagine you were thinking to yourself, "Is that all we're going to learn and practice about these forms of prayer? Isn't there more we could hear and experience than the brief explanation, a practice, and a discussion?" Of course, the answer is yes. Any of these methods of prayer could be explored in-depth over a long period of time through a book study or in an ongoing class. You could offer a weekly prayer experience at the church or in someone's home. Some churches hold an intercessory prayer time or a centering prayer group one morning or evening a week. These groups are open to anyone and often consist of a small core group with others who come when they can. People tell me that even if they are unable to attend, they find joy in knowing that others are in prayer during that time, and they join them in spirit.

An annual prayer retreat is often of interest in a praying congregation. This could take place at the church for a morning or a full day, or at a retreat center for a longer period. The retreat might focus on one form of prayer, offering instruction followed by opportunities to practice individually and as a group. The retreat could offer members the experience of being silent together. They might discover a new depth of fellowship that develops when they simply share space, time, meals, and worship together without conversation.[9] Offering a prayer retreat of any design to church members and to others in the wider community lets people know that prayer is at the heart of this congregation.

If you are teaching prayer in your congregation, open yourself to the spirit, and be guided by the needs of your people. Mix and match the ideas in this book, lengthening some lessons, eliminating others, or placing them in different order.

ACTIVITY 7.1 : FURTHER RESOURCES

If you wish to teach the prayer forms and spiritual practices mentioned at the top of page 136, the following resources may be helpful.

Henri J. M. Nouwen, *Behold the Beauty of the Lord: Praying with Icons,* Notre Dame, Ind.: Ave Maria Press, 1987.

Lauren Artress, *Walking a Sacred Path: Rediscovering the Labyrinth as a Sacred Tool,* New York: Riverhead Books, 1995.

Pat B. Allen, *Art as a Way of Knowing: A Guide to Self Knowledge and Spiritual Fulfillment through Creativity,* Boston: Shambala Press, 1995.

Marjorie J. Thompson, "The Practice of Self-Emptying: Rediscovering the Fast." In *Soul Feast: An Invitation to the Christian Spiritual Life.* Louisville: Westminster John Knox Press, 1995.

Christine D. Pohl, *Making Room: Recovering Hospitality as a Christian Tradition,* Grand Rapids: William B. Eerdmans Publishing Company, 1999.

Ronald Klug, *How to Keep a Spiritual Journal: A Guide to Journal Keeping for Inner Growth and Personal Discovery,* Minneapolis: Augsburg Books, 1993.

You might want to begin with teaching people to pray out loud by including that practice in an existing class or meeting time. You may wish to invite someone to teach and guide members in a form of prayer not discussed here, such as praying with icons, walking the labyrinth, or exploring ways to pray through art. Your congregation may be interested in learning about and practicing fasting, hospitality, journal keeping, or some other spiritual practice.

As you teach prayer and spiritual practices within your congregation and guide the members into a deeper relationship with God, remember that you are not alone. You might want to contact other leaders in other churches who realize that many people come to church searching for a place to learn about prayer, wanting to pray with others, and hoping to hear others talk about prayer. These seekers may not be aware of their longing, but when they find a congregation that meets their unspoken needs, they are likely to stay and become involved. The newcomers will need to be welcomed in with their questions and doubts, experiences and hopes. They may fit into the existing programs, or they may bring new needs and gifts that you had not anticipated. New members, as well as long-time members who are growing in their prayer lives and raising unexpected questions, may make you rethink your programs, begin a process again, or find new ways to encourage the wonder of prayer.

Becoming a praying congregation is not a linear process but a time of unfolding and deepening.

Becoming a praying congregation is not a linear process but a time of unfolding and deepening. There is no particular starting point and no destination. You will find your congregation turning and twisting back on itself, starting and stopping for no apparent reason, and sometimes growing in a direction you had not anticipated. All congregations experience successes and failures along the way. One pastor told about trying to bring prayer into a committee established to raise money and oversee a major addition to the church. "They would have nothing to do with prayer," she said. "They saw it as a waste of time. The members of this committee were task and goal oriented, and they said that prayer was not necessary. However, my early morning Bible study class was willing to learn more about prayer and was eager to include different forms of prayer as part of their time together. And in their time of intercession they prayed for the building project!"

Both leaders and members of the congregation need to be willing to accept that both progress and resistance are part of the process of becoming a praying congregation. If you get discouraged, reach out to others who hold the same vision of church as you do. Share your frustrations and dreams with them. In your own prayer life, ask God for help and courage. Take time to rest in the loving presence of God. And when you get distracted by all the other things a church needs to do besides pray, and you wander away from your desire to be part of a praying congregation, gently bring yourself back to your original intention. Like the

> *Live in the trust that God is waiting for you and always celebrates your return.*

process you encounter in centering prayer, know that you will not be consistent in your attentiveness to God, and consistency is not to be expected. Your task is to pay attention to where you have wandered, acknowledge where you are, and gently bring yourself back to God. No matter how often you stray, live in the trust that God is waiting for you and always celebrates your return. The process of wandering and returning, leaving and coming back, is the faithful practice that turns a church into a praying congregation.

AFTERWORD

In the months since I began writing this book I have been invited to numerous congregations to teach about prayer. The presentations have taken a variety of forms: an educational hour after church, a Saturday morning exploration, a Sunday afternoon to discuss Lenten prayer practices, an evening dialogue around a potluck meal, and in one case, a full-day workshop to discover the many ways we pray. A few presentations had more than fifty people in attendance, and one attracted only seven participants. But no matter the format or the numbers, those who came were eager to talk about prayer, share their experiences and questions, and learn new ways of praying alone and together.

After one event, one woman told me that her husband of twenty years had shared a memory of his grandfather that she had never heard before. Another woman told a group that she wasn't sure why she prayed, because she didn't believe in prayer. A young man said at the end of an afternoon gathering that he realized he was praying much more than he had thought. "I didn't think I was praying at all, because I was not up at dawn and down on my knees."

The people I met and shared with were not unusual. They were women and men from many walks of life ranging in age from 16 to 85. Some had been brought up in praying families, and others had not met prayer until young adulthood. Many were long-time members of the congregation that sponsored the event, but others were newcomers. One woman had just visited the church for the first time that morning and saw the announcement of the presentation in the evening. "I knew I had come to the right place when I saw that people in this church were gathering to talk about prayer," she said.

Like the people, the congregations I visited were not special or set apart from other churches in any way. They were large, medium-sized, and small, rich and poor, growing and declining. They were like churches all over our land and probably similar to the church you are attending or the church you are hoping to find. However, they did have one thing in common: at least one person in the congregation (often a lay person) felt the longing to explore prayer in community, articulated this desire, and then acted to make it happen. That person was like the woman in Jesus' parable who takes a little yeast and mixes it with three measures of flour until all of it is leavened (Matthew 13:33).

Just one person with a vision for what can happen when prayer is at the core of a community is needed for a church to become a praying congregation. One person to request a study group on prayer. One person to ask another how her prayer life is going. One person willing to share an intimate experience of God. One person longing to deepen his prayer life in the company of others. I believe these individuals and others like them are present in all our congregations, eager to break the silence that has surrounded prayer and longing for their churches to become places of prayer.

As a church grows in its commitment to prayer, all difficulties will not disappear nor will all conflicts be resolved. Becoming a praying congregation does not magically create a perfect church. Remember the man who, when asked how his life had changed after he had learned to pray, responded that things

had gotten worse? But he also said that because of his deepened experiences of prayer, he had more courage to face his
difficulties and a deeper faith in God's presence in his life.

So it is with a praying congregation. Issues will still arise
about which people disagree. Changes in leadership will occur,
and not everyone will be happy. Membership may grow or de-
cline, creating new challenges such as the need to revise the
church's mission and ministries. And congregations will probably continue to wrestle with inclusive language, what kind of
music they want to hear, or some other aspect of worship. These
problems will not go away. But members of a praying congregation can ground themselves in God. They can take their
struggles into prayer individually and collectively. They can listen to each other and to God, sharing their hopes and dreams
as well as their doubts and fears. Becoming a praying congregation does not assure a church of any particular outcome, but
a praying congregation has new ways to face difficult decisions
and more options for solving conflicts. The congregation is
grounded in God's loving intention for wholeness and healing,
and through their experiences of prayer, members are more
willing to trust God's presence in all aspects of the life of the
church.

In the week before his crucifixion and resurrection, Jesus
was teaching in the temple in Jerusalem. He asked the people,
"Is it not written, 'My house shall be called a house of prayer
for all the nations'?" (Mark 11:17). As we enter into the spirit
of Holy Week (whatever the season of the year), can we hear
the ancient wisdom in the words of Jesus? Can we be faithful to
God's command to turn our churches into houses of prayer for
all the people? God is calling us to transform our worshiping
communities into praying congregations. May we listen, may
we hear, and may we respond.

Palm Sunday 2005

NOTES

Epigraph

Richard Rohr, *Everything Belongs: The Gift of Contemplative Prayer* (New York: The Crossroad Publishing Company, 2003), 147.

Preface

1. William Lord and John C. Bryan, *Project on the Spiritual Development Needs of Mid-Career Clergy: Report of Findings* (Toronto: Toronto School of Theology, 1999).

Chapter 1, Praying Congregations

1. Eugene H.Peterson, *The Contemplative Pastor: Returning to the Art of Spiritual Direction* (Dallas: Word Publishing, 1989), 100.
2. You can learn more about the ministry of InterPlay at www.bodywisdom.org.

Chapter 3, What Do You Believe about Prayer?

1. Ann Ulanov and Barry Ulanov, *Primary Speech: A Psychology of Prayer* (Atlanta: John Knox Press, 1982).
2. Fleming H. Revell, ed., *The Practice of the Presence of God with Spiritual Maxims by Brother Lawrence* (Grand Rapids: Spire Books, 1967).

Chapter 4, Images of God

1. Tony Hendra, *Father Joe: The Man Who Saved My Soul* (New York: Random House, 2004), 57.
2. Marcus J. Borg, *The God We Never Knew* (San Francisco: Harper Collins Publishing, 1997), 32.
3. Marcus J. Borg, *The Heart of Christianity: Rediscovering a* *Life of Faith* (San Francisco: Harper Collins Publishing, 2003), 66–67.

Chapter 5, Praying All Ways and Always

1. Keith Beasley-Topliffe, *The Upper Room Dictionary of Christian Spiritual Formation* (Nashville: Upper Room Books, 2003), 35.
2. Marjorie J. Thompson, *Soul Feast: An Invitation to the Christian Spiritual Life* (Louisville: Westminster John Knox Press, 1995), 142.
3. Spiritual Directors International has a list of spiritual directors in your area. You can contact them through www.sdiworld.org. Request the name of your local contact person, who will provide some names for you to consider.

Chapter 6, Becoming a Teacher of Prayer

1. William H. Willimon, "Back to the Burning Bush," *The Christian Century* 119 (April 24–May 1, 2002): 7.
2. Ibid.
3. Marjorie J. Thompson, "Rooted and Grounded in Christ: A Pastoral Letter on Spiritual Leadership," in *Leading from the Center* (Nashville: The General Board of Discipleship, The United Methodist Church, Spring 2001), 3.
4. For more information on the compassionate observer see my article "The Compassionate Observer: An Experiential Model for Formation," *Presence: The Journal of Spiritual Directors International* 4, no. 3 (1998): 24–33.

5. Steve Doughty, *To Walk in Integrity: Spiritual Leadership in Times of Crisis* (Nashville: Upper Room Books, 2004), 30.

6. An excellent resource for authentic teaching is Parker J. Palmer, *The Courage to Teach: Exploring the Inner Landscape of a Teacher's Life* (San Francisco: Jossey-Bass, 1998).

7. Parker J. Palmer, *Let Your Life Speak: Listening for the Voice of Vocation* (San Francisco: Jossey-Bass, 2000), 88.

Chapter 7, Teaching Prayer Forms and Spiritual Practices

1. Douglas V. Steere, "Intercession: Caring for Souls," *Weavings: A Journal of the Christian Spiritual Life* 4, no. 2 (1989): 19.

2. Thanks to Rita Burgland, who taught me most of these movements.

3. Beasley-Topliffe, ed., *The Upper Room Dictionary of Christian Spiritual Formation*, 265.

4. Joseph D. Driskill, *Protestant Spiritual Exercises: Theology, History and Practice* (Harrisburg, Penn.: Morehouse Publishing, 1999), 95–96.

5. Quoted by John M. Buchanan, "Grace Notes," *The Christian Century* 121 (September 7, 2004): 3.

6. David Steindl-Rast, *Gratefulness: The Heart of Prayer* (New York: Paulist Press, 1984), back cover.

7. Hendra, *Father Joe*, 202.

8. Richard J. Foster, *Celebration of Discipline: The Path to Spiritual Growth* (San Francisco: Harper Collins, 1998), 136–139.

9. Jane E. Vennard, *Be Still: Designing and Leading Contemplative Retreats* (Bethesda, Md.: The Alban Institute, 2000).